more to me.

dedication

**For my family, who has taught me
from the beginning that there is so much
more to me.**

My dad, who has always shown our family the
unconditional love of The Father here on earth and lives
with honesty, integrity, and conviction. You've always
believed in each of us and encouraged me to follow my
dreams, and for that, I am grateful.

My mom, who has gently taught me that life is about
having the courage to be vulnerable, and lives with faith,
empathy, and strength in the midst of trials. Thank you for
your consistent and unfailing support – especially for
reading every single draft of this book!

My sister Anneliesse, who has always been there for me;
thank you for caring and loving so fiercely and fully. Your
compassionate heart is one of your best qualities, and you
have shown your strength by stepping forward into your
life with such grace. I'm so proud of the woman you
already are, and all that you are accomplishing.

My sister Evie, who has brought our family such joy, light,
and laughter. Your thoughtfulness, maturity, and
compassion is truly remarkable, and it's so amazing to see
the talent and heart God placed within you beginning to
really take root and bloom. I'm so proud of the young
woman you are becoming.

My favorite dog and cat, Sophia and Stella, thank you for
bringing our family comfort and snuggling up next to me
while I wrote this book! (Although Stella really wanted to
help me write this by walking on the keyboard…)

more to me.

discovering your freedom through identity

AN INTERACTIVE JOURNEY
& PRAYER JOURNAL
BASED ON THE LYRICS
OF THE SONG "MORE TO ME"

Cristabelle Braden

contents

introduction

The night that I wrote the song *"More To Me"*, I felt incredibly broken. Sitting alone at the piano on Christmas Eve, with twinkle lights glowing, praying and crying and praying and crying, I just couldn't shake the feeling that I would never ever get past my circumstances.

Even though I knew "logically" that God had a plan for me, I didn't feel it in my heart. But I wanted to much to hold onto that hope. I wanted so much to believe it. I wanted so much for there to be something more than this hurt... something more than this pain... something more than my every day reality.

This emotion had to get out, because it was too painful to keep bottled up. And the best way I know how to express emotion is through music. As I started singing, it was like a release. As the tears flowed, the notes floated into the air, and the presence of God became tangible. Alone in my bedroom that night, the atmosphere shifted... and I felt the love of God completely envelope me.

*"The Lord is close to the brokenhearted
and saves those who are crushed in spirit."
(Psalm 34:18 NIV)*

I can still remember so clearly the first moment I sang out the words, *"I know there's more to me than the wreckage you see...".* In that moment, tears were streaming down my face, and in that moment I felt a glimmer of hope. It was like by singing out that sentence, somewhere in my heart I was making the choice to believe that there could - maybe - possibly - somehow - be more to me than this.

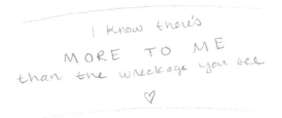

Sometimes we have to choose to believe even when we don't feel it. The words came quick: *"there's more to be... I'm still on the journey".* This was my declaration. Even when my life felt like a mess, I chose to believe there was still more to come. There had to be.

This song is my heart completely bared. Asking hard questions, such as: *"Who have I become?" "Where do I belong?" "When did I become my own worst enemy?"*

This song is so deeply personal that I honestly thought I would never play it for anyone, ever. But the Lord started to speak into my heart that it needed to be shared. In a rush of emotion, I realized that I am not the only one who feels this way. I'm not the only one who struggles with hard questions. I'm not the only one who has ached in loneliness and cried so deep that my entire body shakes.

If you can relate to any of this feeling of inadequacy, the feeling of not knowing, and the feeling of being defined by everything wrong in your life, I want you to know that you are not alone in this. And it's okay to struggle and cry.

I know what it is to feel completely defined by my circumstances. When my brain injury happened, I had to re-learn things that were once simple, such as taking a shower and getting dressed. I had trouble holding conversations and struggled with intense short-term memory loss. Doctors told my family I may never even finish high school, and we had to face the reality that things really may never get better. It seemed absurd to dream big when I couldn't even get through the day. I thought I would never, ever get past this brain injury.

Through this process, I've personally experienced the beauty that comes in learning how God sees so much more to me than my situation! I'm writing this now from a place of hope and healing. Early on after my brain injury, doctors said I might not finish high school… but I went on to get my bachelors degree, graduating with high honors! Even though I still struggle with my brain injury, every day I see the Lord taking me forward a little bit at a time.

Not only that, but I never wrote a song before my brain injury, and now I tour all over the country singing and sharing about hope, and have an organization for brain injury awareness and support called "Hope After Head Injury". These are things that we never would have seen coming!

When God put the idea for this book on my heart, nearly two years after originally writing the song, my initial reaction was fear... I didn't know what to write! I didn't know what to say! Yes, I write songs all the time, but I've never considered myself an actual author. Actually, I really struggled through college with writing papers because of the symptoms of my brain injury. The idea of writing an entire book seemed so overwhelming. But I just couldn't shake the feeling that this message needs to be shared. So I am writing this book for every person who has ever felt defined by their situation, struggles, and hurts.

This isn't a book about me. It doesn't chronicle my story. This is a book for you!

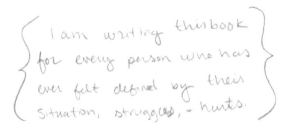

I am writing this book for every person who has ever felt defined by their situation, struggles, - hurts.

This interactive journey is designed to be on your own timing at your own pace. Each section goes through a lyric from the song *"More To Me"*. I share my heart behind the lyrics and some of my favorite Bible verses. It has intentionally been written conversationally, because it's straight from my heart to yours.

Each section has questions and places to write, so that you can personally reflect and spend time seeking God's heart for your life. I even wrote quotes out in my own handwriting throughout the book – we are on this journey together!

I hope and pray this journey will lead you a little bit closer to knowing just how much you are truly loved by God. There is so much more to you!

In love,
Cristabelle

more to me.
MUSIC AND LYRICS BY CRISTABELLE BRADEN

Who have I become? Wrapped up in a memory
Where do I belong? It's been so long and every time
I try to make sense of anything, I find that I'm stressed bout everything
This isn't who I used to be

When the waves came and when the storm raged
Found myself falling into the ground
When the wind blew, that's when it fell through
And I don't know how to turn it around
I know there's more to me than the wreckage you see
There's more to be, I'm still on the journey

When did I become my own worst enemy?
Where did I go wrong and start to think that every time
I make a mistake on anything, I'll never come back, I'll never be
The person that I want to be

When the waves came and when the storm raged
Found myself falling into the ground
When the wind blew, that's when it fell through
And I don't know how to turn it around
I know there's more to me than the wreckage you see
There's more to be, I'm still on the journey

I've had some hard days, had some sleepless nights
And I've been afraid of giving up the fight
I'm more than what happened to me
But it's still part of my story

When the waves came and when the storm raged
Found myself falling into the ground
When the wind blew, that's when it fell through
And I don't know how to turn it around
I know there's more to me than the wreckage you see
There's more to be, I'm still on the journey

one: created for a purpose

"who have I become…"
-lyric from "more to me"

It can be so hard to have faith in the middle of a broken and seemingly hopeless situation. Maybe you've been hurt by a failed relationship. Someone you thought would be in your life forever just… left.

Maybe you've been hurt by an injury or chronic health condition. It can be so hard to keep perspective while struggling every day with symptoms and physical pain.

Maybe you've been hurt by addiction, abuse, a financial blow, or maybe a loss in your family… whatever it may be, you can't find your way out.

How do we find hope in the middle of confusion? How do we even know what we're feeling when everything is just so hard? How do we keep going when nothing makes sense?

I remember asking myself *"Who have I become?"*, because I would look in the mirror, feeling like a failure, an empty shell of a person, not even recognizing myself anymore.

If you're in the thick of it, I want you to know that there is so much more to you than this situation. Whatever your hurt, Jesus is right there with arms open wide to love you for everything that you are and all you were created to be.

We can get this perception in our mind that having faith means that you don't worry. Oh, how that couldn't be further from the truth... but in our anxious minds, we start to believe that we have to get ourselves somewhat together in order for God to work in our lives. Or, we think that we have to "follow the rules" or never mess up in order to call ourselves a Christian. We start to feel that we have to be "religious" or have been raised in church in order to know God and for Him to care, or we feel shame for having been raised in the church and now questioning our faith.

If you've felt any of these ways, know that you are not alone, and it's okay to struggle. But, also know that you do not have to get yourself together to have faith.

Faith begins with simply having an open heart to God. That's it. Don't overthink it… just breathe in His presence. God loves you because of who He is, not because of anything you've done or haven't done.

What does having faith mean to you?

_____

_____

_____

_____

_____

_____

_____

_____

Put your hand on your heart. Feel that pulse? Now take a deep breath. Feel that air filling your lungs? If you have a beat in your heart and a breath in your lungs, God is not done with you yet. There is a purpose for your life. You can't give up now!

faith begins with simply having an open heart to God

FEARFULLY AND WONDERFULLY MADE

When I've struggled with feeling unworthy of God and lost in this world, I start by going back to how and why I was created. It's a way to remind myself that there is a purpose for my life, even if it doesn't feel like it right now.

> *"So God created man in his own image."*
> *(Genesis 1:27 NIV)*

God created us in His image and likeness, which is part of how we are connected to Him and how He deeply understands us in return.

Not only did God create you in His image, but He defined and paid attention to every single detail of you individually:

> *"For you created my inmost being;*
> *you knit me together in my mother's womb.*
> *I praise you because I am fearfully and*
> *wonderfully made; your works are wonderful,*
> *I know that full well."*
> *(Psalm 139:13-14 NIV)*

You have been fearfully and wonderfully made! This means that every single piece of you has been knit together with reverence, beauty, and awe. Every characteristic of your personality and every facet of your heart has been placed inside of you with care and with intention.

There is a purpose to your every breath. There is a reason you are exactly who you are. You are the only person like you!

God paid attention to every little detail when He created you. What does it mean to you that you are fearfully and wonderfully made?

_____

_____

_____

_____

_____

_____

_____

_____

_____

_____

_____

_____

YOU ARE GOD'S MASTERPIECE

God created you and breathed life into you, specifically, because He loves YOU so much!

> *"For we are his workmanship, created in Christ Jesus for good works, which God prepared beforehand, that we should walk in them."*
> *(Ephesians 2:10 NIV)*

You are His workmanship. I love how different translations of the Bible phrase that verse… the ESV says we are His "handiwork", and the NLT says we are His "masterpiece". Just take a moment to think on that for a second… God looks at YOU and calls you His masterpiece. The same God who created the stars and galaxies created YOU!

No matter what has happened in your life… there is purpose to you being here, at this time. And no matter what situation you are facing today, you are alive, and you are here to see another day. That is a victory in itself.

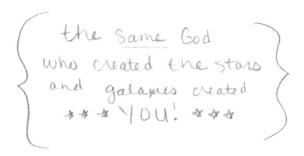

Knowing that God created you with a purpose,
simply start a conversation with Him.

_____

_____

_____

_____

_____

_____

_____

_____

_____

_____

_____

_____

_____

_____

_____

_____

_____

MORE TO YOU

Knowing who you were truly created to be will change your life. When the storms come, we can stand firm knowing that God created us for a purpose, with a plan for our lives already set in motion!

There is more to you because you have been created with a purpose!

two: it's okay to struggle

"wrapped up in a memory…
-lyric from "more to me"

Every single one of us has a story. We all have things we carry with us; things that weigh us down that you can't see on the outside. Your heart, your soul, your deepest loves and your deepest fears sit far beneath the surface.

Because much of our journey is not visible, it can inevitably create a disconnect. You can go to school, or work, or church, and smile and greet everyone… then come right home and cry yourself to sleep.

The truth is, none of us will ever be perfect. We can't always have it all together. There are times when we fall apart. There are times when we struggle, cry, and scream, and there are times when all we can see is the pain in front of us.

And that's okay.

=

IT'S OKAY TO EXPRESS EMOTION

There are so many examples in the Bible of suffering, questioning, and trying to find Truth in the middle of tragedy. Psalm 42 is one of my favorite passages showing this struggle.

The book of Psalms is found in the Old Testament of the Bible, and it's full of poetry, song lyrics, prophecy, and so much truth! There is something about the expression of poetry and music that can touch deep into our hearts, which is why I love the Psalms so much.

Psalm 42 is recorded as written by the Sons of Korah, so we know where it came from but we do not know the specific name of the author. I love the first part of this Psalm, because it shows us that it's okay to question, hurt, and struggle.

> *"As the deer pants for streams of water,*
> *so my soul pants for you, my God.*
> *My soul thirsts for God, for the living God.*
> *When can I go and meet with God?"*
> *(Psalm 42:1-2 NIV)*

The honest outpouring written in this Psalm so long ago is still relevant today. The author writes of a desperate need to find God, but not knowing where to find Him. There is that question, *"When can I go and meet with God?"*

The image of thirsting is important. Think of how you feel when you are thirsty and dehydrated. The author compares his feelings to a deer, desperately thirsty and searching for a stream of water to drink and find some relief. This relates to how our souls can feel - parched and dry and thirsty. Have you been there?

You want something to change, but you don't know how to do it. You know God is somehow close, but you honestly can't feel Him. You want to get closer to God, but you don't feel worthy of Him.

I've had so many times when I've known God was somehow there, but I didn't know how to connect with Him whatsoever.

It's like my emotions and my desperation were clouding and overshadowing the truth of His presence. All I could see in those moments were my fears, and I couldn't figure out how to even begin to connect with God in the middle of all of this – because my emotions were just so strong.

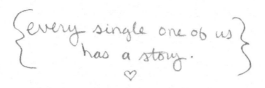

{ every single one of us has a story. ♡ }

What emotions do you experience that make it feel harder to connect with God?

Express and simply list out some of your feelings below.

_____

_____

_____

_____

_____

_____

_____

_____

_____

_____

_____

_____

_____

IT'S OKAY TO QUESTION

After expressing his desperation for something to change, the author goes on to say:

> *"My tears have been my food day and night,*
> *while people say to me all day long,*
> *"Where is your God?"*
> *(Psalm 42:3 NIV)*

The author writes, *"my tears have been my food"...* what a striking image of heartbreak. I can imagine that the author was writing this in a place of being so heartbroken that he couldn't even eat; the only food he had consumed was his tears – all day and all night. So many of us have been in that place of heartbreak.

As the author of this Psalm writes about his constant tears, he begins to express how others are judging and mocking him in the middle of his pain. Have you ever felt misunderstood and judged in the middle of a heartbreaking situation? It can be so hard to express ourselves. The author writes how others see his tears and proceed to mock him, saying *"Where is your God?"* – as if to imply that there's no way that God can possibly be there in the middle of this much pain.

But the truth is… we don't always know how to answer that question, because if we are honest, we are also wondering where God could possibly be in the midst of our trials.

I've asked myself so many times where God is in the middle of my pain. I have then felt shame and guilt for even questioning where God is. If I couldn't feel God's love, I felt like it meant that I somehow failed as a Christian. But that's not true at all. I've learned that when I've felt guilty for questioning, I was actually missing the point of God's love for me.

God knows that we will sometimes feel this way, and He is prepared to meet our needs and answer us. I believe that's why these types of questions were put right there in the Bible for us to read and know that we are not alone in these feelings, so that we can clearly see and know that it's okay to question. We don't have to feel guilty about it! There is actually an entire book of the Bible called "Lamentations", which is simply an account of questioning and crying out to God! God is showing us that we have freedom to question. You are allowed to ask God where He is. He is big enough to handle all of your questions and more.

There is no shame in questioning where God is in the middle of your pain; have security in knowing it's okay for you to have uncertainty. God loves you so much! He is not mad at you. He would rather you question and cry out to Him than push those thoughts away. You have the freedom to express yourself.

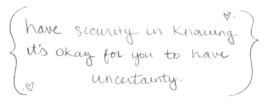

have security in knowing it's okay for you to have uncertainty.

Have you ever felt guilty for questioning God?

_____

_____

_____

How does it make you feel knowing that you
have the freedom to question and ask God
where He is in your pain?

_____

_____

_____

_____

What is something you want to ask God? Write
your prayer asking Him here. No matter what
it is, He listens and He loves you so much.

_____

_____

_____

_____

_____

_____

WRAPPED UP IN A MEMORY

Directly after expressing struggles with constant tears and questioning, the author of this Psalm writes:

"These things I remember
as I pour out my soul:
how I used to go to the house of God
under the protection of the Mighty One
with shouts of joy and praise
among the festive throng.
(Psalm 42:4 NIV)

I love how this Psalm expresses how even good memories can be painful. When I wrote the lyrics, *"Who have I become? Wrapped up in a memory...",* I was struggling with figuring out how to let go of my past hurts and move forward. The memories felt so far away, but I couldn't help but re-live them and dwell on them.

So many of us struggle with being wrapped up in our memories. Maybe you're remembering happier times. When your present reality is so hard, it can hurt so much to think about how much easier things used to be. All you want is to go back to those times... but you can't. It's just different now. And that hurts so much.

Or maybe you are struggling with the memories of something very hard that has happened. Things are better now, but you can't figure out how to move forward, because there is a huge disconnect between your daily life and the memory of what has hurt you.

It's okay to miss the past, but we can't control what has already happened to us. All we can do is focus on how we are going to react and keep going every day. In order to move forward, we have to begin to recognize and express our emotions instead of pushing them down.

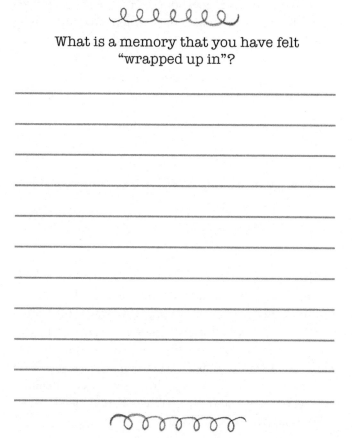

**What is a memory that you have felt
"wrapped up in"?**

IT'S OKAY TO CRY

After expressing his struggle with memories, the author writes in verse five:

> *"Why, my soul, are you downcast?*
> *Why so disturbed within me?"*
> *(Psalm 42:5a NIV)*

Have you ever questioned *"Why am I feeling this way?"* I've had so many days when any little thing could just bring out the tears… and I couldn't even figure out why. I just feel broken. My tendency when I have felt these emotions is to think that I "shouldn't" be feeling this way.

In order to move forward, we have to begin to recognize and express our emotions instead of pushing them down. ♡

Just like the author of this Psalm, I begin to question why I'm even feeling this way, and then I start to feel guilty for my emotions. This relates to when we apologize to others when we start to cry. Have you ever done that? The thing is… we shouldn't feel guilty for how we feel. It's okay to cry. Feelings are very real, and if you've experienced these emotions, you are not alone.

The author of this Psalm continues to write, still speaking directly to his soul:

"Put your hope in God,
for I will yet praise him,
my Savior and my God."
(Psalm 42:5b NIV)

Even in the middle of all of that pain and sorrow, the author of this Psalm speaks directly to his soul.

Even in the middle of this pain and heartbreak, he is holding onto hope in God that someday things will get better and he might begin to find a way out of this pain.

This example shows us that when we hope in God instead of in our circumstances, we will have a clearer picture of how to move forward.

I fully believe that God put these passages from Psalm 42 in His Word in order for us to know it's okay to feel, it's okay to cry, and it's okay to question. Through Psalm 42, and other Psalms about struggles, the Lord has shown me that I have the freedom to struggle with this. He has given me a freedom within my pain.

These feelings are something we have to go through, but we don't have to go through alone.

YOUR EMOTIONS HAVE PURPOSE

God has created us to have emotion, which is part of being made in His image and likeness… because God experiences emotions too. That's why we feel things so deeply. The Bible is full of descriptions of the full range of God's emotions; I've selected just a few examples here to show you how the Father, Son, and Spirit all feel deeply.

God the Father is filled with emotion for you, He experiences deep longing and compassion for you:

> *"Yet the Lord longs to be gracious to you;*
> *therefore he will rise up to show you compassion."*
> *(Isaiah 30:18a NIV)*

From what we know about the life of Jesus, it's so clear that He experiences emotions very deeply. Here, Jesus verbalizes His feelings to His disciples before going to pray in the Garden of Gethsemane:

> *"Then he said to them, "My soul is overwhelmed*
> *with sorrow to the point of death. Stay here and*
> *keep watch with me." (Matthew 26:38 NIV)*

We also know that because God came as a man in the form of Jesus, He experienced the physical side of human emotion:

> *"Jesus wept."*
> *(John 11:35 NIV)*

The Holy Spirit also experiences emotion; we know from this verse that the Spirit of God can experience grief:

"And do not grieve the Holy Spirit of God, with whom you were sealed for the day of redemption." *(Ephesians 4:30 NIV)*

Even in the middle of our pain, Holy Spirit never leaves us and understands our sorrow.

When we recognize that we are created in the image of God in His fullness, our emotions can serve as a vehicle to help to bring us closer to His heart.

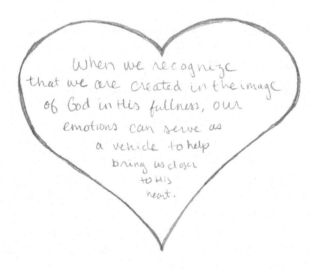

Now that you see that God has emotions like you do, begin to express your heart freely to Him.

If you struggle with putting things into words, begin by singing, drawing, or painting something while praying and asking Him to work your way through this emotion. Then, once you've expressed yourself in creativity, sit down and write a prayer.

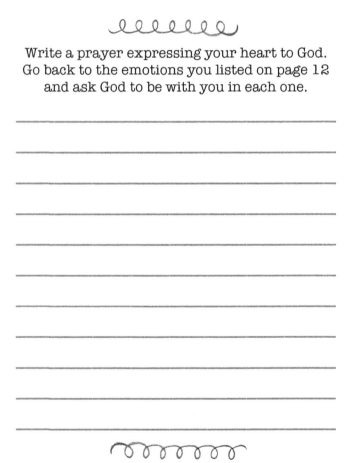

Write a prayer expressing your heart to God. Go back to the emotions you listed on page 12 and ask God to be with you in each one.

WITH A LITTLE FAITH

Having uncertainties in life doesn't mean your faith will not work. It just gives you the opportunity to press in even more and seek the Lord in the midst of your questions and emotions.

By placing our hope in God, even in the middle of these emotions and confusion, we make the choice to choose light over darkness. We make the choice to not give up, even when we can't feel it. We make the choice to have faith. Jesus tells us:

> *"Truly I tell you, if you have faith as small as*
> *a mustard seed, you can say to this mountain,*
> *'Move from here to there,' and it will move.*
> *Nothing will be impossible for you."*
> *(Matthew 17:20b NIV)*

Have you ever seen a mustard seed? It's a very, very tiny seed. Jesus is using this illustration to show us that all we need is a little tiny bit of faith!

Jesus has given us the freedom to question while still keeping our faith – because all we need is faith as small as a mustard seed. God loves you so much that He will take that small seed of faith and move a mountain in front of you. Nothing will be impossible for you!

Write a prayer asking God to help you move forward in the midst of your emotion.

Simply by the act of writing this prayer, you are planting that small seed of faith.

_____

_____

_____

_____

_____

_____

_____

_____

_____

_____

_____

MORE TO YOU

The struggles you go through are part of your story. They shape you, but they do not define you in your identity. Breathe deeply today knowing that God is with you in the middle of your every emotion, and that you are fully known and fully loved.

There is so much more to you than your struggles.

three: peace beyond understanding

"where do I belong? it's been so long and every time I try to make sense of anything, I find that I'm stressed 'bout everything..."
-lyric from "more to me"

It can hit at any moment... that feeling where you can't get enough of a breath in... mind spiraling out of control... heart beating fast.

Anything can trigger it... an offhand comment made casually by a friend or acquaintance... an image passing across your screen as you're scrolling on social media... a scene in a tv show or movie... even just your own thoughts.

Anxiety.

It's a battle so many of us face.

And it's a very real thing.

What goes through your mind when something in your life goes wrong? Do you stress? Do you worry? Do you get anxious often?

_____

_____

_____

_____

_____

_____

_____

What is a recent time that you've felt stressed?

_____

_____

_____

_____

_____

_____

_____

GOD CARES FOR YOU

This is one of my go-to passages from the Bible when I'm feeling anxious. Here, Jesus is teaching during the Sermon on the Mount:

> *"Therefore I tell you, do not be anxious about your life, what you will eat or what you will drink, nor about your body, what you will put on. Is not life more than food, and the body more than clothing? Look at the birds of the air: they neither sow nor reap nor gather into barns, and yet your heavenly Father feeds them. Are you not of more value than they?" (Matthew 6:25-26 ESV)*

Next time you go outside and see birds in the sky, think about how God has given them all they need. You are worth so much more to God than the birds - you were created in His image, for a purpose!

> *"And which of you by being anxious can add a single hour to his span of life?"(Matthew 6:27 ESV)*

Jesus is basically reminding us that worrying doesn't do anything to help our situation. It's the simplest phrase, but it's really hard to keep that perspective. Even knowing this, my natural tendency is to worry first! My head can know one thing to be true, but my heart can still feel anxious. I believe that Jesus took the time to talk about feeling anxious because He knows we struggle with this.

Jesus knows how our hearts and our heads don't always line up, so He speaks directly to our hearts. In His great love and understanding, Jesus knew we would need this assurance of the Father's love and provision. When we allow the truth of these words to not only resonate in our minds, but also sink deep into our heart, we can begin to find freedom from our anxiety. Next, Jesus says:

> *"And why are you anxious about clothing?*
> *Consider the lilies of the field, how they grow: they*
> *neither toil nor spin, yet I tell you, even Solomon*
> *in all his glory was not arrayed like one of these.*
> *But if God so clothes the grass of the field, which*
> *today is alive and tomorrow is thrown into the*
> *oven, will he not much more clothe you, O you of*
> *little faith?" (Matthew 6:28-30 ESV)*

Think about how you would talk to a friend who is dealing with anxiety. You would talk kindly, softly, gently, to help calm them. That's how this passage feels in my heart... the words of Jesus so gently whispering into my soul.

God's understanding of our hearts is so great and beautiful, because He created us with these emotions. Here, Jesus' gentle, loving voice is kindly correcting me on my little faith... and He's absolutely right. When emotions are going crazy, having faith can be the last thing on my mind and sometimes the last thing I want to hear. In my anxious heart, I'm getting in this downward spiral thinking about how many things are so OUT of control!

Jesus gently reminds us of His love for us by asking, if God takes care of the birds and the flowers, won't he take care of you so much more? You, whom God created individually and loves so very deeply?

Care for yourself with the love of Jesus. Talk to yourself the way you would talk to a friend.

Write an encouraging message to yourself, to remind you how much God cares for you and loves you.

_____

_____

_____

_____

_____

_____

Now, take this message and write it on a post it note or piece of paper. Put it up somewhere that you see every day as a gentle reminder of how much God truly cares for you!

SEEKING GOD FIRST

God knows your needs and is prepared and ready to meet each of them:

> *"Therefore do not be anxious, saying, 'What shall we eat?' or 'What shall we drink?' or 'What shall we wear?' For the Gentiles seek after all these things, and your heavenly Father knows that you need them all." (Matthew 6:31-32 ESV)*

Jesus takes the time to address our anxiety because He knows we need the reminder of how much God cares for us. He urges to know just how deep the Father's love runs for us, so that we can have confident faith in knowing that God is taking care of us.

God knows your needs and is prepared and ready to meet each of them.

❀ ❀ ❀

When Jesus says "do not be anxious", He gives us something else to put our energy into instead:

> *"But seek first the kingdom of God and his righteousness, and all these things will be added to you." (Matthew 6:33 ESV)*

Instead of worrying first, Jesus gently reminds us that we can seek Him first. We can grow in knowing Him deeper, and as we do, our anxious heart will be lifted up off our chest.

{ instead of worrying first, Jesus gently reminds us that we can seek Him first. ♡ }

We can't be so inward focused that we forget that God made a way for us to move past this with His love and provision. We have the freedom to look to God, even in the middle of our anxiety!

"Therefore do not be anxious about tomorrow, for tomorrow will be anxious for itself. Sufficient for the day is its own trouble." (Matthew 6:34 ESV)

This verse reminds us to be present in each day. Because, again, Jesus knows our hearts… our tendency to worry so much about the future that we forget to live in the present. Instead of worrying our days away, we can truly take each day and live within that day.

Another one of my favorite passages related to anxiety comes from Philippians, a letter written by the Apostle Paul to the early church at Phillipi:

> *"Do not be anxious about anything, but in*
> *everything by prayer and supplication with*
> *thanksgiving let your requests be made known to*
> *God." (Philippians 4:6 ESV)*

When those anxious moments come your way, instead of allowing the fear and despair to cloud your mind, simply lift your thoughts up to God. Prayer doesn't have to be this formal thing at church where you say fancy words, it can just be giving each thought to Him.

Prayer is simply a connection with God.

It's about reminding yourself that He is there in the midst of this anxiety, and inviting Him into your heart to be a part of this moment. A prayer can be as simple as just starting a conversation with God.

> When those anxious moments
> come your way, instead of
> allowing the fear and despair
> to cloud your mind, simply
> lift your thoughts upto God.
> ↑

You don't have to know why you feel anxious,
but one thing that can help you get through
these moments is to pray.
Just start a conversation with God, and as you
write, begin to tell Him how you feel.

_____

_____

_____

_____

_____

_____

Next, ask Jesus to help you learn how to begin
to seek Him first in your anxious moments.

_____

_____

_____

_____

_____

FREEDOM TO NOT UNDERSTAND

When I get in those anxious moments, my heart overtakes my head – and sometimes, the last thing I'm thinking about is praying. I start to downward spiral. Everything begins to feel extreme and these thoughts start creeping in… saying I will never be good enough, that nobody cares about me, that I should just give up, and more.

It's scary and so hard when these lies begin to circle my mind, because I really feel like I'll never get out of my situation. Everything piles on top of itself, and it gets worse and worse. I believe that is exactly why the Lord led Paul to remind us to pray in our anxious moments; because God knows how we desperately need that reminder to seek Him first! The very next verse in this passage from Philippians reads:

"And the peace of God, which surpasses all understanding, will guard your hearts and your minds in Christ Jesus." (Philippians 4:7 ESV)

The peace of God surpasses all understanding… which means I have the freedom to not understand. I don't have to understand where the anxiety is coming from, and I don't have to understand this situation in my life. We don't have to understand the circumstances, we just live through them.

I love this verse because it shows how the Holy Spirit can speak peace into your heart in these anxious moments, and guard your heart and mind from feeling so out of control.

I just love the image of God guarding my heart and mind… it's like the Holy Spirit is there as a club bouncer outside my heart keeping out the false thoughts! *"Insecurity? Doubt? Fear? Shame? I see you trying to get in… but sorry, you're not on the list!"* Yes, it's a funny little image, but this is actually what God can do for our hearts. He can guard us with peace beyond our own understanding.

When everything feels out of your control, it's still right in God's control – which is why seeking Him first in prayer is so powerful. Remember that God can actually do something about your situation even when you can't… and He loves you so much that He is prepared and ready to meet your needs and act on your behalf!

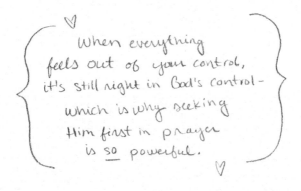

When everything
feels out of your control,
it's still right in God's control –
which is why seeking
Him first in prayer
is *so* powerful.

Instead of holding on to your anxieties, list
them out below, and one by one, ask God to help
you begin to let them go.

_____

_____

_____

_____

_____

_____

_____

_____

_____

_____

_____

_____

_____

_____

_____

_____

_____

_____

MORE TO YOU

If you struggle with anxiety, don't put yourself down in those moments; instead, seek God first. Jesus loves you so much and He understands your anxiety.

There is so much more to you than these anxieties and worries because you were created by a loving God who has an amazing plan for your life!

four: unchanging identity

"this isn't who I used to be...
-lyric from "more to me"

Have you ever looked in the mirror and didn't even recognize yourself? It's so easy to lose yourself in the middle of a hard season. And it's so easy to be so unkind to yourself. Every day you feel a little more lost. Every day, you lose a little more hope. Every day, you feel more and more like you're completely falling apart.

How can there be more to me when I don't even know who "me" is anymore?

We tend to define ourselves by our personality, our likes and dislikes, our family situation, our finances, our job, and our education. We also tend to define ourselves by our mistakes, our failings, and our current circumstances. We create these shiny online versions of ourselves with all these things listed and perfectly filtered photos, as if to say to the world: *"this is who I am."* But have you ever posted something and immediately felt insecure because you didn't get very many "likes" or comments? Have you ever had an "on this day" memory appear at the top of your feed, and it just made your heart sink because you feel like you can't live up to that version of yourself anymore?

Have you defined yourself by something that has happened to you? What was it?

_____

_____

_____

_____

_____

_____

_____

So many of us can truthfully say "I'm not who I was", whether it's one year ago or ten years ago. We learn, we grow, we love, we grieve, and as a result our personalities and likes and dislikes naturally evolve and change.

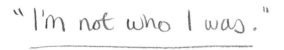

"I'm not who I was."

How can I be myself when my moods change with each day? How can I be myself when I look in the mirror and see a stranger? How can I be myself when I don't have anything left to dig into? How can I be myself when my entire world is falling apart?

Is it hard for you to know how to be yourself?

_____

_____

_____

_____

_____

What in your life has impacted the way you view yourself?

_____

_____

_____

_____

_____

YOUR TRUE IDENTITY

There will be seasons of your life when you feel strong and secure and confident in knowing who you are. There will also be seasons of your life when every day is filled with tears and struggling. In order for our identity to stand through the seasons, it has to be based in something that never changes.

"Jesus Christ is the same yesterday and today and forever." (Hebrews 13:8)

Jesus never changes, and we can have confidence that His love for us will never change.

"See what kind of love the Father has given to us, that we should be called children of God; and so we are." (1 John 3:1a ESV)

The only part of my identity that never changes is my identity that is found in the love God has for me. Our true value is not in anything we have done, or haven't done... our value is in the Father's love for us. He calls us His children.

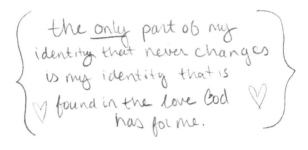

the only part of my
identity that never changes
is my identity that is
found in the love God
has for me.

Truly "being yourself" doesn't have anything to do with your personality, your likes, your dislikes, your circumstances… it doesn't have to do with anything that can change.

Being yourself is simply knowing that you were created and you are loved with an everlasting love.

I want to challenge you to define yourself differently. Not by who you were yesterday, not by who you are today, not by any part of your identity that shifts and changes. In the middle of your hurts, define yourself as a child of God. Loved, secure, and with a purpose for your life. Next time you look in the mirror, look right into your own eyes, take a deep breath, and say out loud to yourself, *"I am a beloved child of God."* Repeat that as many times as you need to hear it.

When we step into our identity as true children of God, we begin to see how much more to us there really is. The pressure is all off. You were created for a purpose. Your life has meaning. Your identity is as a child of God. Nothing and no one can take that away from you.

"I am a beloved child of God."

Write your prayer asking God to help you to
begin to see yourself through His eyes,
as a beloved child of God.

_____

_____

_____

_____

_____

_____

_____

_____

_____

_____

_____

_____

_____

_____

_____

_____

_____

MORE TO YOU

We don't have to live up to these unrealistic expectations in our heads any longer. Instead, we have the freedom to simply be ourselves... knowing that we are more, because we were created to be more.

There is more to you because you are not defined by your view of yourself. You are simply defined as a child of God!

five: when I am afraid…

"when the waves came, and when the storm raged, found myself falling into the ground…"
-lyric from "more to me"

Fear can creep up when you least expect, in so many little ways. Have you ever been afraid of what other people think of you? Afraid of losing someone that's important to you? Maybe you're afraid of failing a test, or that you can't pay your bills? Have you ever been afraid that your best might not be good enough?

If you experience fear in some way on a daily basis, then... you're probably human. We all experience fear in so many different ways. But when the storm hits, fear can become crippling. It's usually not rational… fear can just be this overwhelming feeling that we can't always pinpoint. How do we move past our fear when we feel like we're drowning and can't even come up for air?

Something that can help us begin to move forward is to recognize where our fears are coming from, and what it is that triggers us feeling afraid.

What makes you feel afraid?

(Just be honest with yourself here. Nothing is too big or to small. Every fear is valid.)

_____

_____

_____

_____

_____

_____

_____

When throughout the day do you find yourself dealing with fear?

_____

_____

_____

_____

_____

_____

_____

GOD IS WITH YOU IN YOUR FEAR

When I feel afraid, one of the first places I go is Psalm 23:

> "The Lord is my shepherd; I shall not want.
> He makes me lie down in green pastures.
> He leads me beside still waters.
> He restores my soul.
> He leads me in paths of righteousness
> for his name's sake.
> Even though I walk through the
> valley of the shadow of death,
> I will fear no evil, for you are with me;
> your rod and your staff, they comfort me."
> (Psalm 23:1-4 ESV)

Take a deep breath and read that passage one more time.

This Psalm was written by David, and it's one of the most well known and beautiful passages in the Bible. We can find comfort in the truth that is found in this Psalm, knowing we are never alone!

When it feels like everything is at it's absolute worst... when you've hit rock bottom... in *the valley of the shadow of death...* God is right there with you, reaching out in love to comfort your heart in these moments of fear. His Spirit is close. He restores your soul. He leads you moment by moment.

The rest of Psalm 23 reads:

"You prepare a table before me
in the presence of my enemies;
you anoint my head with oil;
my cup overflows.
Surely goodness and mercy shall follow me
all the days of my life,
and I shall dwell in the house of the Lord forever."
(Psalm 23:5-6 ESV)

Not only is God with you in your darkest valley of fear, but He is actively bringing you restoration. Even in the middle of your worst situation, in the presence of your enemies, God is blessing you with His goodness and mercy.

This means that when everything seems to be going wrong, and when it feels like everyone is against you, God is with you and He is for you. You are His beloved child.

> Not only is God with you in your darkest valley of fear, but He is actively bringing you restoration.

Here is another reminder that God is with us in our fear:

> *"Have I not commanded you? Be strong and courageous. Do not be frightened, and do not be dismayed, for the LORD your God is with you wherever you go." (Joshua 1:9 ESV)*

We are only able to replace our fear and dismay with strength and courage when we recognize that God is with us wherever we go.

Whatever you are going through, whatever giant you are facing, whatever situation you are worried about... God reminds us that we do not need to fear, because He is right there working in the midst of our circumstances! Holy Spirit can strengthen us moment by moment as we step forward and face our fears.

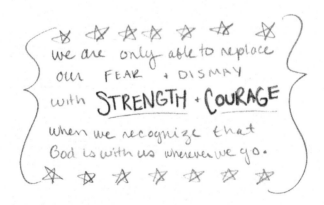

How does it make you feel to know that God with you in your fears, already working to bring you restoration?

_____

_____

_____

_____

_____

_____

_____

_____

_____

_____

_____

_____

_____

_____

_____

_____

_____

THIS FEAR WILL NOT CONSUME YOU

When dealing with fear, another place I like to go is Psalm 56, another Psalm of David:

> *"When I am afraid, I put my trust in You. In God, whose word I praise, in God I trust; I shall not be afraid. What can flesh do to me?"*
> *(Psalm 56:3-4 ESV)*

The thing that strikes me the most here is that this verse says "when" I am afraid... not "if" I am afraid. That is an important distinction to show that fear really does happen. What a comfort to know that our fear is real... it's not something that can be brushed off. There will be many moments in our lives when we feel afraid. But it's what we do with our fear that matters most.

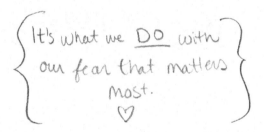

It's what we DO with our fear that matters most. ♡

Do we allow the fear to consume us? Or do we choose to look to God, who is right there with us, even while we're shaking in our boots?

When we are afraid, we are focusing on the consequences of any given situation. We are afraid of what may happen... We are afraid of the unknown. But even when our future is unknown, the love of God can be intimately known.

> *"There is no fear in love, but perfect love casts out fear. For fear has to do with punishment, and whoever fears has not been perfected in love." (1 John 4:18 ESV)*

Perfect love - the love that God has for us - that is what can cast this fear out of our hearts. So, not only is God with us in our fears, but it goes deeper... we have the assurance that God can actually shine the fear out of our hearts with His powerful love!

This also goes back to the last section, where Jesus reminds us to seek Him first in our anxiety. It's all connected; seeking God first is part of how we experience this perfect love!

Thinking about the fears you listed out at the start of this section (page 50), write your prayer asking God to show you His love for you in a personal way, and to help you start to move past your fear.

_____

_____

_____

_____

_____

_____

_____

_____

_____

_____

_____

_____

_____

_____

MORE TO YOU

If you're afraid today, soak in His love.
God knows the depths of your heart. He knows your
deepest fears, and He is with you in every single one
of them. He is with you in the storm. He is with you
in the valley. Breathe it in. Step out… trust in Jesus…
you are safe in His love. This fear will not define you.

**There is so much more to you than your fears,
because God's perfect love is right there to drive
out fear, comfort you, and restore you!**

six: the depths of love

"when the wind blew, that's when it fell through, and I don't know how to turn it around..."
-lyric from "more to me"

Have you ever felt so broken that you felt like you weren't able to be loved? Pushing people away because you feel that your "stuff" is too much for anyone else to deal with? Feeling forgotten and afraid to be vulnerable because of those who have betrayed you? Putting on a fake smile because you have absolutely no idea how to even express yourself?

I've been there... and the deeper I would hide into myself, the more I began to focus on all of my flaws, and the more walls went up. How could there possibly be more to me than this? How could anyone actually love me in this mess?

Our view of love becomes tainted when we get hurt. Our culture has watered down the term "love" to mean just about any sort of affection. We use "love" towards our family and friends, but we also say the same thing about food and material items. We can say we are in "love" in a romantic relationship, only to have the person choose to walk out of our lives.

My experience on this earth taught me that love changes. Love leaves me. Love betrays me. Love breaks me. I'm left wondering... *"What does "love" really mean anyway?"*

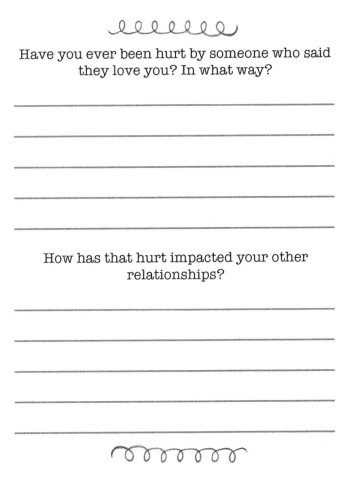

Have you ever been hurt by someone who said they love you? In what way?

_____

_____

_____

_____

_____

How has that hurt impacted your other relationships?

_____

_____

_____

_____

THE LOVE GOD HAS FOR YOU

When we have been wounded and let down by love in our lives, it can be really hard to comprehend just how much God truly loves us. It's not intentional, but it's so easy to get to a place where your heart feels so beat up that you have no idea what love really means. In those moments of emptiness, the love of God can feel so far away.

Have you ever felt so removed from love that hearing someone say "Jesus loves you" doesn't even make a difference, or even seem possible? If you can relate to this, then you're not alone.

I've been in a place where I felt so far removed from God's love that just the idea of trying to pray in my tears made no sense to me. I was just surviving in my dark world, day in and day out. Every time I heard someone say "Jesus loves you," what I was really thinking inside is *"I don't even know what that means."*

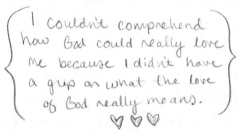

I couldn't comprehend how God could really love me because I felt so unlovable and unworthy. I couldn't comprehend how God could really love me because I didn't have a grip on what the love of God really means.

This is one of the most well-known passages about love in the Bible:

> "Love is patient, love is kind. It does not envy, it does not boast, it is not proud. It does not dishonor others, it is not self-seeking, it is not easily angered, it keeps no record of wrongs. Love does not delight in evil but rejoices with the truth. It always protects, always trusts, always hopes, always perseveres. Love never fails."
> *(1 Corinthians 13:4-8a NIV)*

You might have heard this passage before, but take a moment to read it again. Really take some time to reflect on this definition of love and think about what each phrase means. This is a description of the true and perfect love God has for you.

God's love is not like man's love. It's not able to bend and it's not able to break. God's love doesn't have to be earned. It is constant, consistent, and unfailing.

> "For I am convinced that neither death nor life, neither angels nor demons, neither the present nor the future, nor any powers, neither height nor depth, nor anything else in all creation, will be able to separate us from the love of God that is in Christ Jesus our Lord." *(Romans 8:38-39 NIV)*

God will never leave us, and absolutely nothing can separate us from His love. Even when you don't feel it, God's love is right there, and it isn't dependent on the love having to be returned:

"This is love: not that we loved God, but that he loved us..." (1 John 4:10 NIV)

This is really important, because our feelings are always changing. Think about it: how many different emotions and moods do you experience in a day? Even within the span of 15 minutes, I know that my mood can change drastically!

I've also experienced relationships that grow and change... my feelings for people can change over time, depending on what has happened. Especially if they have hurt me. It's really hard to love someone who doesn't love you in the same way. Really, really hard. That's why we have to understand how different the love of God is for us. We could never love God in the same way as He loves us; yet He loves us unconditionally, beautifully, and perfectly.

God's love for you is constant, and it's not dependent on your feelings or perception of it. It doesn't change, no matter what happens, no matter what we do. The truth is, His love is there whether you know it or not.

"Not we have loved God, but that he loved us."

What a beautiful assurance.

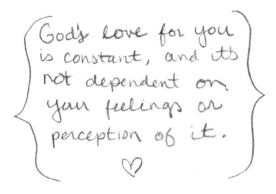

God's love for you
is constant, and its
not dependent on
your feelings or
perception of it.
♡

God's love doesn't have to be earned. Reflect on
that, compared to past experiences and hurts
with imperfect love from people.

GOD'S LOVE IN ACTION

Here is the next part of that last verse we read:

> *"This is love: not that we loved God, but that he loved us and sent his Son as an atoning sacrifice for our sins." (1 John 4:10 NIV)*

Not only has God chosen to love you, but He did something to prove it. God put love into action for you when He sent Jesus to this world to die for you!

> *"For God so loved the world that he gave his one and only Son, that whoever believes in him shall not perish but have eternal life. For God did not send his Son into the world to condemn the world, but to save the world through him."*
> *(John 3:16-17 NIV)*

The love of God can be fully known by the hope we have in Jesus. In the next section, we will explore more of what it means that Jesus came to die for us.

Right now, rest in the assurance of God's love for you. God's perfect love is strong enough to shine out all of your fears and hurts. It's not dependent on anything you've done, or haven't done, but simply on who God is.

Write your prayer asking God to show you more of His love for you. If you have been hurt by an imperfect human love, simply ask God to begin to restore your heart with His perfect love instead.

_____

_____

_____

_____

_____

_____

_____

_____

_____

_____

_____

_____

_____

_____

_____

MORE TO YOU

You can rest today in knowing that you are so incredibly loved by a God that is bigger than you can even imagine. He created you. He chose you. He is for you. And nothing can separate you from His love.

There is more to you because you are perfectly loved by God!

seven: your value in grace

"I know there's more to me than the wreckage you see..."
-lyric from "more to me"

Do you struggle with being hard on yourself? There are so many times I've caught myself throughout the day just beating myself up in my head. I would never, ever say the unkind things I say to myself to another person. When I'm trying so hard to measure up and to please everyone, it never feels like enough. I just continue to put myself down in my heart.

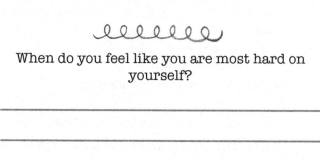

When do you feel like you are most hard on yourself?

_____

_____

_____

Never more deeply do I feel the truth of this verse than when I'm trying to work my way to perfection... and failing:

"For all have sinned and fall short of the glory of God..." (Romans 3:23 NIV)

Oh boy, do I fall short. I see it in myself daily. In those moments of struggle, feeling like I'll never measure up, I forget there is another part to that sentence:

"...and all are justified freely by his grace through the redemption that came by Christ Jesus." (Romans 3:24 ESV)

ALL have sinned and fall short.
ALL are justified freely by His grace.

Falling short doesn't mean that I don't deserve God. Falling short just shows how much I'm loved. God looks at us, even with all our shortcomings, with eyes of love, mercy, and compassion. Even in the middle of our struggles, while we were dead in transgressions (which is just another way to say our sins), God chose to look on us with grace:

"But because of his great love for us, God, who is rich in mercy, made us alive with Christ even when we were dead in transgressions – it is by grace you have been saved." (Ephesians 2:4-5 NIV)

GRACE IS A FREE GIFT

Have you ever received an unexpected gift? Maybe on your birthday, or Christmas morning? It's such an amazing feeling to get a gift. It makes you feel loved, doesn't it? When you get a gift, it's yours for no other reason than someone decided to give it to you. You didn't do anything to earn this gift... you weren't the one that paid for it. You just get to unwrap it and receive it. That is exactly how God gives us salvation:

> *"For it is by grace you have been saved, through faith—and this is not from yourselves, it is the gift of God— not by works, so that no one can boast." (Ephesians 2:8-9 NIV)*

Grace is unmerited favor. It's a gift! We didn't purchase this gift ourselves; Jesus purchased it for us and gave it to us freely.

{ GRACE }
is unmerited favor.

Recognizing this gift has changed my life completely, and it is the reason why I sing, write, and share hope. I can't write a book called "more to me" without writing about this gift that has brought me so much freedom and shown me how much more to me there is! I want to share with you about why this gift is so important, and how incredibly powerful and beautiful it is for our lives. This verse explains why we even need this gift:

> *"For the wages of sin is death, but the free gift of God is eternal life in Christ Jesus our Lord."* (Romans 3:23 NIV)

The wages of sin is death... this means that it would be impossible to get this gift for ourselves.

Think about the world we live in. The headlines. The senseless tragedies. The wars. The killings. It's so much to take in. And besides that, in our own lives, we fall short on a daily basis. We don't mean to, but sometimes we can't help it. Life is so hard and messy because sin has infiltrated our entire existence.

We call it human nature, but it's really the sin we struggle with. Sin is part of human nature, and we can't escape it on our own. All of the pain and struggles, all the emotions and weariness we go through, is a consequence of this fallen and dead world.

Our sins have earned us death, and because of our sins, we are in an debt.

Think about a time you've been in debt... Have you ever borrowed money from someone? Have you ever had to make monthly loan payments? The outstanding debt doesn't just go away. The price has to be paid by someone! It's pretty non-negotiable. The only way to get out of a debt is to pay the price yourself, or to have your loan forgiven. But even loan forgiveness has been paid for by someone; a debt of money doesn't just disappear into thin air. Loan forgiveness just means that the debt has been paid for by whoever has chosen to forgiven the loan.

That's where the free gift comes in.

God looked at this debt we earned and decided to take it upon Himself instead. Jesus signed His own name on the dotted line when He paid the price with His death. The debt that was written in your name has been replaced with the name of Jesus. The moment He died for you the price of death was erased from your record. You are no longer in debt; your record is now spotless and clean.

That is the free gift! It's so amazing. Because Jesus already paid the price, we have forgiveness of our debt of sins and we don't have to die, because the death has already been paid for! Our sins are no longer separating us from life with God – and we can step into the freedom of eternal life!

This is why this gift is so amazing! Our salvation means that we are saved from the death that we deserve because of our sins, and we have access to eternal life as a free gift! If we had to pay the price of death ourselves, there would be no possible way for us to have eternal life. We couldn't buy this gift ourselves. The debt had to be forgiven and paid by someone else in order for you to have life. And Jesus loves you enough to have already done it for you.

JESUS PAID THE PRICE

We looked at the perfect love of God in the last section, and now we can see how beautifully God has put that love into action. God came as a man in the form of Jesus – just so that He could purchase this gift for us. That's how much God loves you! Jesus was able to pay the price of death that we deserved because He lived a life with no sin:

> *"God made him who had no sin to be sin for us, so that in him we might become the righteousness of God." (2 Corinthians 5:21 NIV)*

See – it had to be God in His perfection to pay the price. Someone who had their own debt of death to pay could never take on anyone else's. But because Jesus never sinned, He didn't have his own debt demanding the price of death. Jesus had a clean record, and in love, He chose to fill it with our debt instead.

Because Jesus never sinned, Jesus was able to take every single person's debt upon his pure, clean, spotless record and pay the price for all of us. He became our perfect and holy sacrifice:

> *"He himself bore our sins in his body on the tree, that we might die to sin and live to righteousness. By his wounds you have been healed."*
> *(1 Peter 2:24 ESV)*

In His infinite love for us, Jesus looked at us in all of our mess and said "you are worth it." He voluntarily chose to take our debt and carry the weight of our sins, to the point of death. He looks at you with eyes of love and forgiveness and sees someone worth dying for.

God has fully, completely, and perfectly forgiven your debt through the death of Jesus and given you eternal life as a gift - you do not have to do anything to earn His love.

How does this change the way you view your relationship with Him?

_____

_____

_____

_____

_____

_____

_____

_____

_____

JESUS CHOSE THE CROSS

Knowing you're created and loved by God takes on a whole new meaning when you realize how much Jesus gave up for you.

Jesus was flogged, beaten, stripped, mocked, spit on, and crucified. A crown of thorns was placed on His head. Nails were driven through his hands and feet, and He hung on a cross, suffocating as He slowly died until He couldn't pull Himself up any longer to take a breath. *(read the accounts in Matthew 27, Mark 15, Luke 22, & John 19)*

Crucifixion was the worst death possible in Roman times, and it was meant only for the worst of criminals. Jesus, an innocent man, died the painful death of a criminal in order to completely and fully pay the price of death for you and for me. That is how much God loves you and wants you to experience life!

Every time I really think about what Jesus has done for me, I'm just completely overwhelmed. I didn't deserve this at all. But the love of Jesus is so much greater than my faults, my hurts, my mistakes, my failings... the love of Jesus is so pure and perfect.

Jesus chose the cross for you and for me. Jesus loves you so much that He took every ounce of your pain, your guilt, your shame, your suffering, and He took the burden for you.

This passage about the death of Jesus comes from the Gospel of Matthew, in the New Testament, which is an account of the life of Jesus on this earth. I love this passage because it really shows in detail the magnitude of what happened when Jesus paid the price of death for us. This death was different, it was significant:

> "And when Jesus had cried out again in a loud voice, he gave up his spirit. At that moment the curtain of the temple was torn in two from top to bottom. The earth shook, the rocks split and the tombs broke open. ... When the centurion and those with him who were guarding Jesus saw the earthquake and all that had happened, they were terrified, and exclaimed, "Surely he was the Son of God!" (Matthew 27:50-52a;54 NIV)

The wages of sin is death.

Paid in full.

All because of the love that God has for you.

Jesus went to great lengths to show you His
love and pay the price of death for you. How
does that change your perspective on how you
see and value yourself?

_____

_____

_____

_____

_____

_____

_____

_____

_____

_____

_____

_____

_____

_____

_____

_____

YOUR VALUE IN GRACE

This is another of my favorite passages about God's love for us, coming from Psalm 103, which is another Psalm of David. See what it says:

> *"The Lord is compassionate and gracious,*
> *slow to anger, abounding in love.*
> *He will not always accuse,*
> *nor will he harbor his anger forever;*
> *he does not treat us as our sins deserve*
> *or repay us according to our iniquities."*
> *(Psalm 103:8-10 NIV)*

How amazing is that? God does not treat us as our sins deserve. God does not make us pay the debt on our own. What a clear picture of the way God feels about us. Already, God was revealing to David about His plan for our salvation – about 1000 years before Jesus came to live on earth! And this is just one of the many, many, many prophecies in the Old Testament that perfectly line up with the salvation we have in the sacrifice of Jesus.

I also love how this Psalm shares how God is *"slow to anger, abounding in love"*. We definitely see that abounding love in death of Jesus! Because God looks on us with such grace and compassion, we can be kind to ourselves in those moments when we feel we are failing. God is not mad at you. He loves you. So why are we so hard on ourselves when God looks on us with so much love?

The next part of this Psalm says:

> *"For as high as the heavens are above the earth,*
> *so great is his love for those who fear him;*
> *as far as the east is from the west,*
> *so far has he removed our transgressions from us."*
> *(Psalm 103:11-12 NIV)*

Because of what Jesus did on the cross, your sins have been forgiven. The debt has been cancelled and removed from you - *as far as the east is from the west*. Because of what Jesus did on the cross, we have the freedom to rejoice in grace instead of dwelling in mistakes. As we read in the last section:

> *"For God so loved the world that he gave his one*
> *and only Son, that whoever believes in him shall*
> *not perish but have eternal life. For God did not*
> *send his Son into the world to condemn the world,*
> *but to save the world through him."*
> *(John 3:16-17 NIV)*

Whoever believes in Him no longer has to die, but can have eternal life. This freedom is yours simply through your belief in Jesus! That is the free gift!

Our value is not in anything we have done, or haven't done; our value is in the Father's love for us. Our value is no longer in the debt that we owe, but is found in the gift that has been purchased by the death of Jesus. That is your value in grace.

Write your prayer asking God to show you your true value in grace. Holy Spirit is right with you to comfort you and help you to be kind to yourself instead of dwelling in your mistakes.

Ask Jesus for forgiveness for your sins, and thank Him for what He has done for you on the cross. Thank Jesus for the amazing gift of grace He has given you.

Ask God to help you let go of feeling like you have to earn His love, and to show you just how much He freely loves you.

_____

_____

_____

_____

_____

_____

_____

_____

_____

_____

MORE TO YOU

If you're struggling with feeling inadequate, look to Jesus. There is more to you than the wreckage you see because Jesus has chosen to take every part of it upon Himself. We can truly let go of these hurts when we recognize that we can't do this on our own... and it's already been done.

There is so much more to you because Jesus chose to give Himself up for you.

eight: there's more to be

"there's more to be, I'm still on the journey…"
-lyric from "more to me"

It feels like it's over a lot in our lives, doesn't it? Maybe your finances are struggling and you don't see any possible way to make ends meet this week. Maybe there's a person in your life that left you, and it feels like they took your life and heart with them. Maybe the doctor just gave you a diagnosis that makes your stomach drop. There are many times when we feel like there is no possible way out of a situation in our lives.

When is a time you wanted to give up, because you felt like it was all over in your life?

_____

_____

_____

_____

WHEN IT FEELS LIKE THE END...

The day that Jesus hung on the cross, it felt like it was over. By the world's standards, it was over... His lifeless form hung from a cross. The disciples had watched Him be flogged, beaten, and nailed to a cross. They watched Jesus take His last breath and declare, *"It is finished"*:

> *"When he had received the drink, Jesus said, "It is finished." With that, he bowed his head and gave up his spirit." (John 19:30 NIV)*

Jesus was dead. How can it be more "over" than death? He was then wrapped in burial cloths and placed in a grave, which was then sealed. *(Matthew 27:59-60)* But it didn't end there.

When it felt like it was over, God intervened.

"After the Sabbath, at dawn on the first day of the week, Mary Magdalene and the other Mary went to look at the tomb. There was a violent earthquake, for an angel of the Lord came down from heaven and, going to the tomb, rolled back the stone and sat on it. His appearance was like lightning, and his clothes were white as snow. The guards were so afraid of him that they shook and became like dead men.

The angel said to the women, 'Do not be afraid, for I know that you are looking for Jesus, who was crucified. He is not here; he has risen, just as he said. Come and see the place where he lay. Then go quickly and tell his disciples: 'He has risen from the dead and is going ahead of you into Galilee. There you will see him.' Now I have told you.'

So the women hurried away from the tomb, afraid yet filled with joy, and ran to tell his disciples. Suddenly Jesus met them. 'Greetings,' he said. They came to him, clasped his feet and worshiped him. Then Jesus said to them, 'Do not be afraid. Go and tell my brothers to go to Galilee; there they will see me.'"

(Matthew 28:1-10 NIV)

JESUS DEFEATED DEATH FOR YOU

See, this is where it gets really interesting. We know that Jesus had to die in order to pay the price of death that we earned by our sins. But He didn't stay dead!

Jesus rose from the grave, the power of God on display, and appeared to over 500 eyewitnesses. *(1 Corinthians 15:6)* Jesus is ALIVE, which means that we can have a real relationship with Him! Our freedom isn't just found in His death, but also in His resurrection:

> *"For if we have been united with him in a death like his, we will certainly also be united with him in a resurrection like his. For we know that our old self was crucified with him so that the body ruled by sin might be done away with, that we should no longer be slaves to sin— because anyone who has died has been set free from sin."*
> *(Romans 6:5-7 NIV)*

THIS is the power in grace! We have access to life through the death of Jesus because He took our debt of sin upon Himself and paid the price of death. We are set free from our old selves because Jesus took our place when He died on the cross! We are no longer a slave to our sin, because the price of sin was paid for in the crucifixion. But it didn't stop there!

We are not only united in the death of Jesus, but also in His resurrection. Jesus rose from the grave, victorious over sin and death – and we can experience that victory right along with Him! The next part of that passage reads:

> *"Now if we died with Christ, we believe that we will also live with him. For we know that since Christ was raised from the dead, he cannot die again; death no longer has mastery over him. The death he died, he died to sin once for all; but the life he lives, he lives to God. In the same way, count yourselves dead to sin but alive to God in Christ Jesus." (Romans 6:8-11 NIV)*

Through the death of Jesus, we can count ourselves dead to our sin. The price has been paid. We no longer have to live the way we did before, but we can live with a brand new life!

Through the resurrection of Jesus, we can count ourselves alive to God! Life started in the grave - death has no power over us! We can experience eternal life, right now, with Jesus! The moment you choose to say "yes" to Jesus is the moment your eternal life begins!

Our sin died with Christ and stayed in the grave.
Our freedom rose with Christ and lives forever!

LIFE STARTED IN THE GRAVE.
♡

What does it mean to you to be dead to sin
and alive to God?

_____

_____

_____

_____

_____

_____

_____

Eternal life doesn't start when you go to
Heaven – it starts right now. How does that
change the way you think about your life?

_____

_____

_____

_____

_____

_____

_____

THE SPIRIT LIVING IN YOU

We know that Jesus died for us, and that He rose from the grave by the power of God. Well... think about this: the same Spirit who raised Jesus from the dead lives inside of you:

> *"And if the Spirit of him who raised Jesus from the dead is living in you, he who raised Christ from the dead will also give life to your mortal bodies because of his Spirit who lives in you."* (Romans 8:11 NIV)

Literally... the Holy Spirit of God that raised Jesus from the dead is living inside of YOU! That is how we experience eternal life!

Jesus paid the price of death for us, so we can experience that death to our sins along with Him. Then, Jesus rose from the grave, so we can experience eternal life along with Him! In the same way that He raised Jesus from the dead, the power of the Holy Spirit gives life to you and me!

Not only does Holy Spirit resurrect us into eternal life, but He gives us access to the complete fullness of God's power! A few verses later, Paul writes:

> *"The Spirit you received brought about your adoption to sonship. And by him we cry, 'Abba, Father.'"* (Romans 8:15b NIV)

You are a child of God by the power of the Holy Spirit, who raised Jesus from the dead, and now lives inside of you. This is really powerful stuff! It makes me so excited every time I talk about it! This is the key… this is why there is more to you!

You are made entirely new in Jesus, and because of that, you don't have to be limited by what's happened to you in your life. From the moment you say "yes" to Jesus, you are never the same.

This verse says that the Spirit brings you into adoption as a child of God. Because of what Jesus has done for you, you can have access to the life you were created for in the first place… before sin came in.

You were created as a child of God. Your sin interfered and caused you a debt of death. Jesus paid the price with His death. Jesus rose from the grave, by the power of the Holy Spirit. The moment you believed in Jesus, the Holy Spirit came to live in you to bring you back into fullness as a child of God!

It's so amazing how God brings us into full relationship with Him, and truly gives us new life! We are set free from every part of our past through our life in Jesus. You literally can become an entirely new creation in Christ!

"Therefore, if anyone is in Christ, the new creation has come: The old has gone, the new is here!"
(2 Corinthians 5:17 NIV)

This is even more significant when you know the story of the Apostle Paul, who the Lord used to write that verse. See, Paul wasn't always a follower of Jesus. Before he met Christ, Paul was called Saul, and he was not a happy man. He was a leading persecutor of followers of Jesus who literally hunted, arrested and condemned Christians to death. He was a devout Jew and did not believe in Jesus – he actually hated Christians. Paul said:

> "I persecuted the followers of this Way to their
> death, arresting both men and women and
> throwing them into prison, as the high priest and
> all the Council can themselves testify. I even
> obtained letters from them to their associates in
> Damascus, and went there to bring these people as
> prisoners to Jerusalem to be punished."
> (Acts 22:4-5 NIV)

Then, one day, the Jesus he didn't even believe in appeared to him and spoke to his heart. This encounter with Jesus changed Paul's life completely, and he truly became a new creation in Christ! *(Read the rest of Paul's testimony in Acts 22.)* The man who once persecuted Christians went on to be filled with the power of the Holy Spirit that raised Jesus from the dead! Paul left his old life behind, with all of the shame and guilt that came with it, and stepped into the freedom Jesus purchased for him. And the impact was great; Paul's letters to the early church now make up most of the New Testament.

In another one of Paul's letters, he writes:

"Here is a trustworthy saying that deserves full acceptance: Christ Jesus came into the world to save sinners—of whom I am the worst. But for that very reason I was shown mercy so that in me, the worst of sinners, Christ Jesus might display his immense patience as an example for those who would believe in him and receive eternal life."
(1 Timothy 1:15-16 NIV)

Paul's example shows us how we really can be made entirely new in Christ. Because Jesus died for you and triumphed over death, we have access into eternal life with Him. Let the shackles fall off your heart, knowing you are truly free.

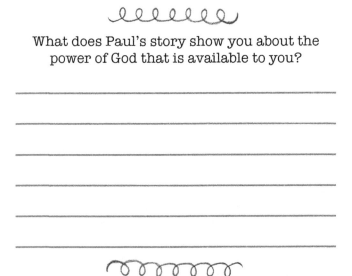

What does Paul's story show you about the power of God that is available to you?

_____

_____

_____

_____

_____

_____

THE FULLNESS OF GOD'S POWER

Eternal life consists of so much more than going to Heaven… eternal life means that we have access to Heaven by the power of the Holy Spirit, right here, right now! We know we have that access into the Kingdom of Heaven, because Jesus was the one who gave it to us when He said:

> *"I will give you the keys of the kingdom of heaven."*
> *(Matthew 16:19 NIV)*

Since Jesus has given us keys to the kingdom of Heaven, we have access to everything God has for us… including the power of the Holy Spirit who raised Jesus from the dead! That's the power that lives in you and in me!

I'm so passionate about sharing this because I've experienced it firsthand in my life. I can't write a book about there being "more to me" without sharing how there really is more to you and me, because God lives inside of us!

This is so important to remember when we are dealing with everyday situations in our lives. The same power that raised Jesus from the dead is living inside of you! We don't have to just talk about our problems; we can see God move right before our eyes:

> *"For the kingdom of God is not a matter of talk but of power." (1 Corinthians 4:20 NIV)*

When we can be aware, moment by moment, of the power of God within us, we will start to see God move in incredible ways! Nothing is impossible for God to handle!

"For nothing will be impossible with God." (Luke 1:37 ESV)

When we're faced with what seems to be our ending, it's just an opportunity for God to make it a new beginning. God can breathe life into your dead situations. Because Jesus rose from the grave, we can experience full freedom in knowing that nothing is impossible for God to do in our lives. You have the fullness of God available to you!

You have access to the fullness of God's power by the Holy Spirit who lives inside of you!

Knowing that Jesus has risen from the dead, and that you have access to that same power by the Holy Spirit, how does that change your perspective on impossibilities in your life?

_____

_____

_____

_____

_____

_____

_____

_____

_____

_____

_____

_____

_____

_____

Even if you have felt like you met your end, God
is already working on your behalf to help you in
your time of need. Write a prayer asking God to
show you a new beginning.

_____

_____

_____

_____

_____

_____

_____

_____

_____

_____

_____

_____

_____

_____

MORE TO YOU

In those moments when it feels like it's over,
remind yourself of this: there is more to be because
Jesus has given you the gift of eternal life with Him.

We can truly see God move and bring about new
beginnings when we realize the true amazing access
we have to Him by the power of Holy Spirit.

**Jesus said there was more to you when He
died for you. And He said there was more to you
when He rose to make you alive with Him
forever!**

nine: freedom is yours

"when did I become my own worst enemy?
where did I go wrong and start to think that
every time I make a mistake on anything, I'll
never come back, I'll never be the person that I
want to be."
-lyric from "more to me"

Have you ever felt so defined by your failings?

Feeling like you'll never ever be able to bounce back from this?

Feeling too ashamed to even talk to other people about it because you don't want to be judged?

Wanting to be a better person, but not knowing how to be?

When I wrote the lyric *"when did I become my own worst enemy"*, I was honestly feeling like every single thing that I was doing was just making it all worse. Every time I tried to reconcile a situation, I felt like I was just getting in deeper. Multiple times a day, the thought *"I hate myself"* would pass through my mind. I didn't even know who I had become. And I didn't know how to be the person that I wanted to be.

What makes you feel as though you are your own worst enemy?

_____

_____

_____

_____

_____

_____

What are some thoughts that go through your head when you are struggling with self-worth?

_____

_____

_____

_____

_____

_____

NO MORE LIES

For a season, I had completely stopped singing because I didn't think that I was worthy to sing worship songs if I was this broken inside. And, if you've ever met me recently or been to a show, you know that is a really big deal for me... cause I pretty much live and breathe music! But I had begun to internalize things so badly that I couldn't even sing or write any songs.

I had just gone through a really hard time, when so many different things came at me at once. The song "More To Me" is one of the first that I wrote coming out of that season, when I was finally able to begin expressing myself again. I honestly did feel like my own worst enemy.

I had started to believe that because I had messed up so bad, I had broken my trust with God and I thought that I could never get back to a relationship with Him that was any good. I felt too broken and "stained" to be called a Christian. My perception of grace was completely messed up... because I had lost touch with the love God had for me. I started to live like I had to earn grace. I was telling myself lies every day... and I know I'm not the only one.

If salvation is our free gift, why do we live like we have to do something to earn it?

Why do we treat our salvation like it is a store transaction rather than a free gift?

When I felt like I messed up, whether it was a big or a small thing, my automatic thought pattern had a tendency to turn to guilt and self-condemnation. Then I started to feel like I was letting God down and like I was unworthy of His love. I had to remind myself of this:

> *"This is love: not that we loved God, but that he loved us and sent his Son as an atoning sacrifice for our sins." (1 John 4:10 NIV)*

God's love for me has nothing to do with what I've done or haven't done, and everything to do with who He is. And if my salvation is truly a free gift… nothing I've ever done or haven't done could have given it to me. Since we didn't do anything to earn our salvation, how could anything we do lose it? This gift is yours. No more lies about your value in grace.

God's love for me has NOTHING to do with what I've done, or haven't done, and EVERYTHING to do with who He is.

♡

THE VOICE OF THE SHEPHERD

Remember when we read Psalm 23, back in section five? We read about how the Lord is our shepherd, and He is with us, so we don't have to fear in our darkest valley. Here in John 10, Jesus shares this about being our shepherd:

> *"When he has brought out all his own, he goes on ahead of them, and his sheep follow him because they know his voice. But they will never follow a stranger; in fact, they will run away from him because they do not recognize a stranger's voice." (John 10:4-5 NIV)*

Whenever a shepherd tends to his flock, the sheep know the shepherd's voice, because they know who takes care of them. But when a stranger comes, the sheep get scared and run away because they know it's not their shepherd.

Jesus uses the metaphor of Himself being the Shepherd, to illustrate how we follow Him when we know His voice. And Jesus also points out the voice of the stranger.

This tells me that we always have two voices coming at us: the voice of the Shepherd, and the voice of the stranger.

The voice of the Shepherd is a voice of love, of familiarity, of truth, of kindness, of mercy, tending to our needs and bringing us closer to Him.

The voice of the stranger is a voice of condemnation, of shame, of insecurity, of fear, of anxiety, accusing us and telling us we'll never be anything more than this.

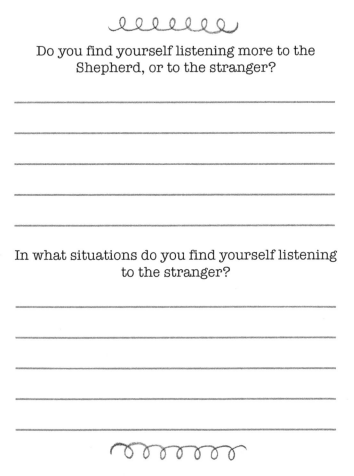

Do you find yourself listening more to the Shepherd, or to the stranger?

_____

_____

_____

_____

_____

In what situations do you find yourself listening to the stranger?

_____

_____

_____

_____

_____

We are not supposed to know the voice of the stranger; we are supposed to run from it. But some of us have allowed the stranger to become our shepherd.

We tend to listen to the voice that's telling us that we're not worth anything, more than we listen to the voice that's telling us how loved we are.

> We are not supposed to know the voice of the Stranger, we are supposed to run from it... but some of us have allowed the stranger to become our shepherd.

The stranger wants us to sit in our shame and never get out of it. The stranger wants us to hate ourselves and live in loneliness. I felt like my own worst enemy because I was listening to this voice in my head telling me that I was never going to be more than this.

I've had to learn that not all of our thoughts are actually coming from us; some are placed there by the voice of the stranger. The enemy, Satan, is very real, and he conspires against the ones that God loves:

> *"Be alert and of sober mind. Your enemy the devil prowls around like a roaring lion looking for someone to devour."*
> *(1 Peter 5:8 NIV)*

Every day, we have a choice as to which voice we are going to listen to. Next time you're tempted to condemn yourself, speak out in truth: *"I am a beloved child of God."* This will help to drive out those lying thoughts telling you that you're not worth anything. Simply ask the voice of the Shepherd to come in and help you.

Write a prayer asking the Lord to help you to get to know His voice on a deeper level. Ask Him to restore and replace the lies that attack you with the gentle truth of His everlasting love for you.

_____

_____

_____

_____

_____

_____

_____

_____

_____

_____

_____

LIFE TO THE FULL

Further down in John 10, while He is still talking about being our Shepherd, Jesus shares this:

> *"The thief comes only to steal and kill and destroy; I have come that they may have life, and have it to the full." (John 10:10 NIV)*

Jesus came for us so that we could have a full life. But we have to know and recognize that the enemy is desperately trying to keep us from it. We know that Jesus triumphed over sin and death when he died for us to pay our debt and rose from the grave. Jesus gives us the free gift of eternal life in its fullness.

The stranger, the enemy, is a thief who is trying to steal your free gift. But he can't really touch it… because it's yours! You already have life to the full! All the enemy can do is feed you lies to try and convince you that this gift is not actually yours. But the enemy can never take your gift away from you.

It comes in the small things… the condemning thoughts that creep in, the frustrating situations, all these little things that add up and then really get your heart. But you have to know that even in your doubts and fears, nothing and no one can take away from you what the Almighty God in Heaven has given! No amount of lies can take your freedom away from you.

Remember – the same power that raised Jesus from the dead is inside of you! Holy Spirit is with you in each moment, to help you withstand and to remind you of the freedom you truly have in Jesus.

Your Shepherd is with you every single step of the way, speaking love over His flock with a kind, caring, gentle voice.

Write a prayer of thanksgiving for the freedom you have in Jesus. The enemy can't touch you! Even if it's hard to see it right now, you have full life available to you! Stand on the truth of that promise. Thank God for the love He has for you, and praise Him for His power and strength.

_____

_____

_____

_____

_____

_____

_____

_____

_____

_____

FREEDOM IS YOURS

Being a Christian doesn't mean that you have it all together. Yes, we will mess up. Yes, we get ourselves in situations. Yes, we make mistakes. I've found that my tendencies in those moments is to freeze up and start to feel like I'll never, ever, get out of this.

Our thought patterns automatically turn to guilt... and that's one of the reasons why we begin to feel defined by our circumstances. But we can't forget that we are set free! When Jesus died, our sins died with him on the cross:

> *"...canceling the record of debt that stood against us with its legal demands. This he set aside, nailing it to the cross." (Colossians 2:13-14 ESV)*

Jesus has paid the price and cancelled the record of debt against us! Every single mistake and sin was nailed to the cross, and there it stood as our Lord's blood flowed down. So now that we are free, let's start to live like it! We condemn ourselves, when there is truly only freedom:

> *"Therefore, there is now no condemnation for those who are in Christ Jesus, because through Christ Jesus the law of the Spirit who gives life has set you free from the law of sin and death." (Romans 8:1-2 NIV)*

How does it change the way you view yourself
to know that there is no condemnation for
those who are in Jesus?

_____

_____

_____

_____

_____

_____

"It is for freedom that Christ has set us free. Stand firm, then, and do not let yourselves be burdened again by a yoke of slavery." (Galatians 5:1 NIV)

The truth of what Jesus has done for us on the cross is so much stronger than our feelings of inadequacy. You are not your own worst enemy. I am not my own worst enemy. But we can certainly feel like it sometimes.

It's okay if you have been struggling with listening to the voice of the stranger. I've been there. But remember the freedom that you already have. It's never too late to return to the voice of the Shepherd who knows your soul and loves you so much!

"For you were straying like sheep, but have now returned to the Shepherd and Overseer of your souls." (1 Peter 2:25 ESV)

Next time those lies try to creep into your mind… lies that are saying you are not good enough, you haven't done enough, you've failed somehow… remind yourself of your true identity as a beloved child of God, redeemed by the blood of Christ. If you are free in Christ, the enemy can't touch you. So stop listening to the lies. Walk confidently, knowing that you are truly free.

Write a reminder to yourself of the freedom you already have in Christ:

_____

_____

_____

_____

_____

_____

_____

Now, take this message and write it on a post it note or piece of paper. Put it up somewhere that you see every day as a reminder of the powerful freedom you have!

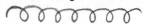

MORE TO YOU

When you struggle with lies telling you that you're not enough, remind yourself of the price Jesus paid for you. Remind yourself of the loving voice of the Shepherd, speaking truth over your heart!

You are a new creation, and there is no condemnation for those who are in Christ Jesus. Freedom means that you can live out each moment in this confidence!

There is more to you because freedom is yours!

ten: finding rest

"I've had some hard days, had some sleepless nights…"
-lyric from "more to me"

When going through a deeply emotional season, it can really affect the quality of your rest. One of the worst feelings is to toss and turn at night, and keep glancing at the clock, dreading each passing hour, realizing it's getting later and later and you're no closer to falling asleep. Hard days can lead to sleepless nights.

What is it that makes you sleepless or restless at night?

_____

_____

_____

_____

YOUR TEARS MATTER TO GOD

Psalm 56 is one of my favorites, because in it, David writes from such a place of honesty in struggles and pain:

"You have kept count of my tossings; put my tears in Your bottle. Are they not in your book?"
(Psalm 56:8 ESV)

Have you ever thought about God collecting your tears? When I first read that, it really spoke to my heart and showed me that every single moment of our pain is important to Him.

Every toss. Every turn. Every tear.

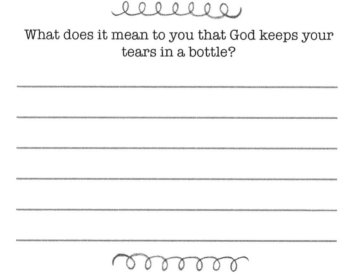

What does it mean to you that God keeps your tears in a bottle?

_____

_____

_____

_____

_____

_____

REST FOR YOUR SOUL

Jesus knows we are weary and burdened. He understands our needs. And in those moments, He offers us His rest:

> *"Come to me, all you who are weary and burdened, and I will give you rest. Take my yoke upon you and learn from me, for I am gentle and humble in heart, and you will find rest for your souls. For my yoke is easy and my burden is light."*
> *(Matthew 11:28-30)*

When Jesus talks about rest, He isn't talking about sleep. There is a connection between rest and sleep, but they are two different things.

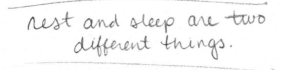

Sleep is something that our bodies physically need. It rejuvenates us and helps us heal in our natural state.

Rest is something that gives you peace, hope, and a sense of relief. Jesus says that when we come to Him, we will find rest for our souls. Our soul is really our mind, our intellect, and our emotions.

What is it that makes your soul feel heavy and burdened?

When we find rest for our souls, we will inevitably sleep in so much more peace.

"In peace I will both lie down and sleep;
for you alone, O Lord, make me dwell in safety."
(Psalm 4:8 ESV)

We can fully rest, knowing that we are safe in His loving arms. We can lie down and sleep in peace when we come to Him and find rest for our souls.

For those moments when all you feel is the weight of your burdens… come and lay it at the feet of Jesus and find your rest.

Your feelings are valid. It's okay to cry. It's okay to hurt. Don't ever feel like you can't feel, or that you "shouldn't" be feeling any certain way. The Bible shows us that it's okay to experience these emotions. The presence of the Holy Spirit never leaves you… gently coming close in your moments of despair, as He lovingly collects each tear. Nothing escapes His perfect hand.

> *"He heals the brokenhearted*
> *and binds up their wounds.*
> *He determines the number of the stars;*
> *he gives to all of them their names."*
> *(Psalm 147:3-4 ESV)*

In these few verses from Psalm 147, we can see how God determines the number of stars in this vast universe, yet also cares about each one of us personally!

The same God who created the universe reaches out with all of the power of Heaven to comfort you in your time of need.

God is both infinitely great and intimately close to each one of us. He reaches deep into our hearts to heal our broken hearts and bind up our wounds. Every single one of our hurts matters to God.

The next verse reads:

"Great is our Lord, and abundant in power;
his understanding is beyond measure."
(Psalm 147:5 ESV)

God understands your struggles, beyond measure.
And He's right there with you.

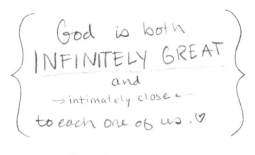

God is both
INFINITELY GREAT
and
→ intimately close ←
to each one of us. ♡

How does it impact your heart to know that the
same God who determines the number of stars
reaches close to heal your broken heart?

_____

_____

_____

_____

_____

_____

SIMPLY COME

Sometimes we feel afraid to come to God to talk to Him or ask Him for things. But you are not bothering God with your problems. God's love is not like mans love; you are not a problem to Jesus. Put that out of your mind right now. You are not an inconvenience to Him.

You can freely come to the Father and express your hurts without fear of punishment, shame, or anger:

> *"The Lord is compassionate and gracious,*
> *slow to anger, abounding in love."*
> *(Psalm 103:8 NIV)*

God's perfect love for you is big enough to cover every single one of your struggles, and you have to understand that He WANTS to take them from you. He WANTS to guide you through it!

You are worth so much more to God than you know. This isn't just that you're not bothering Him… it's so much more than that. Jesus rejoices at the sound of your voice crying out to Him. He is filled with such love for you that it overflows by the power of the Holy Spirit!

Now, Jesus simply asks you to come to Him and receive the love He has for you. You don't need any special words. Just your heart.

> When we lay our burdens
> at the feet of Jesus,
> we trade our burdens
> for His rest. ♥ ⩗⩗

When we lay our burdens at the feet of Jesus, we trade our burdens for His rest. We can have confidence in coming to God with anything and everything:

> *"This is the confidence we have in approaching God: that if we ask anything according to his will, he hears us. And if we know that he hears us— whatever we ask—we know that we have what we asked of him." (1 John 5:14-15 NIV)*

We don't have to worry about bothering our Father, because He wants to listen and give us what we ask of Him! You are God's beloved child. He smiles at you and looks on you with such compassion and love. He cares about every single one of your tears. He has such passion for you that Jesus chose to die in order that you may live!

Have confidence in knowing that Jesus has asked you to come to Him in such love. Come, lay down your burdens, and find your rest.

Come to Jesus with a prayer to ask Him to
trade your burdens for His rest.

Take all of those things you wrote out earlier in
the section (pg 113-116) and simply pray over
each one, asking God to bring you freedom.

Have confidence in asking anything of God –
He is available to you because He loves you!

_____

_____

_____

_____

_____

_____

_____

_____

_____

_____

_____

_____

_____

MORE TO YOU

Jesus says to simply come, and you will find rest for your soul. Rest in this assurance of His love for you... God is with you today, in whatever You're facing. You are so loved!

There is so much more to you because God cares about every single part of you intimately!

eleven: fighting for you

"and I've been afraid of giving up the fight…"
-lyric from "more to me"

Emotional exhaustion and physical exhaustion can go hand in hand. When life is hard, and nothing makes sense, and you have so many days in a row of sleepless nights, you can begin to feel exhausted by everything. And then, one day you wake up and you're not sure if you can hold on any longer.

I went through a season of extreme weariness in my own soul. The tears and fear gripped me.

I began to dread each passing day because every single day it got harder, not easier. I was so afraid of the uncertainties that came against me every day. I felt like I couldn't hang on any longer, but I was scared to let go.

I thought that if I let go, I wouldn't be able to keep any parts of my life together.

Even though I had no energy left inside of me to hold on, I knew I had to keep fighting somehow. I had to keep going, trying to make it work in my own strength, because I was so afraid that letting go would mean that I would fall and may never be able to get back up.

Afraid of giving up the fight.

When do you most feel like giving up the fight?

_____

_____

_____

_____

_____

_____

_____

_____

_____

_____

_____

GOD IS FIGHTING FOR YOU

One day when I was feeling that way, I started to panic. Anxiety gripped my heart, my chest tightened, and my breathing sped up. I just couldn't hold on anymore. I completely broke down and right in that moment, I was on the verge of completely giving up.

In the moment of my breakdown, Holy Spirit came and in a still, small voice, spoke these words:

"I'm fighting for you."

That simple statement caught me off guard and completely shook me to my core.

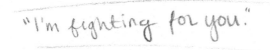

I had been putting all my energy in trying to fight for myself, without giving a second thought to the fact that God was right there fighting for me all along. In a rush of emotion, freedom hit my heart.

Somehow, we get this idea in our minds that we have to do certain things in order to measure up. We think that we have to do something in order for God to fight for us. I know that I've certainly felt that way.

I heard this phrase somewhere and took it to heart, *"God helps those who help themselves."* Have you ever heard that?

Well, let me start by saying that phrase is nowhere in the Bible. It's a lie. But at one point, I believed it. I truly thought that I had to do something in order for God to do something for me.

I felt so low and so broken that I couldn't understand how in the world God could even WANT to work on my behalf, when I couldn't even fight for it myself.

I couldn't understand how God could even WANT to work on my behalf, when I couldn't even fight this battle for myself.

I couldn't understand how in the world God would want to come into my broken mess, especially since I was the one who kept making mistakes and failing at every turn.

But in the middle of my mess, God spoke:

"I'm fighting for you."

GOD GOES BEFORE YOU

This promise of God fighting for us is found many places in the Bible, but my favorite verse on this comes from Exodus 14 when Moses spoke to the Israelites on their way out of Egypt.

The people of Israel were running, gripped with fear with the Egyptian army chasing them. They came to the edge of the sea, nowhere left to run. There was no way they could fight this battle for themselves… they were not warriors, and the Egyptian army was strong. The Bible tells us that the people truly believed they were going to be attacked and die right there.

In the middle of this terrifying moment, Moses spoke:

> *"The Lord will fight for you,*
> *you need only to be still."*
> *(Exodus 14:14 NIV)*

After Moses spoke this out, the Lord parted the Red Sea and the Israelites passed through safely on dry land and the Egyptian army was swallowed up in the sea.

God showed up and fought this battle for them. He made a way where there seemed to be no way.

129

The same God that delivered His people out of Egypt and parted the Red Sea that day is right with you, fighting your battles for you:

"The Lord your God, who is going before you, will fight for you, as he did for you in Egypt, before your very eyes." (Deuteronomy 1:30 NIV)

Before we even try, God is already at work! He is not surprised by our circumstances; rather, He is already there, going before us and is already working on our behalf! God goes before us and is ready to work a miracle in our darkest hour, just like He did at the parting of the Red Sea.

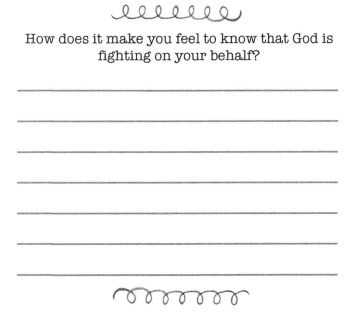

How does it make you feel to know that God is fighting on your behalf?

_____

_____

_____

_____

_____

_____

_____

Every time I've tried to fight on my own, it's always left me exhausted.

We get these ideas in our minds:

The Lord will fight for you… if you fight for yourself.
The Lord will fight for you… if you read your Bible today.
The Lord will fight for you… if you go to church every week.
The Lord will fight for you… if you held it together today.
The Lord will fight for you… if you don't make a mistake.
The Lord will fight for you… if _____.

Have you ever thought to yourself that you had to do something for God, in order for Him to be fighting for you? What was it?

_____

_____

_____

_____

_____

_____

_____

_____

YOU NEED ONLY TO BE STILL

We all have certain things that we feel like we SHOULD be doing... but that's where we get it wrong. Jesus fought for you on the cross, and He won the battle in the grave. He will continue to fight for you every single day of your life!

> JESUS FOUGHT FOR YOU ON THE CROSS — AND HE WON THE BATTLE IN THE GRAVE.

Remember your value in grace and the price Jesus paid on the cross for you. Remember there is no condemnation for those who are in Jesus. The Bible does not say that we have to do anything for God to fight for us. It actually says the complete opposite:

> *"The Lord will fight for you,*
> *you need only to be still."*
> *(Exodus 14:14 NIV)*

Take a deep breath and read that again. You only need to be still... which is actually the opposite of doing anything!

> *"Be still, and know that I am God."*
> *(Psalm 46:10a NIV)*

Simply be still and receive. Freedom comes when we realize that our victory is found in what God has already done for us, and not in what we are trying to do for ourselves.

freedom comes when we realize our **VICTORY** is found in what God has already done for us, and not in what we are trying to do for ourselves.

How does it impact your heart to know that God is already fighting for you, and all you have to do is be still?

GOD IS FOR YOU

The same God who created the heavens and the earth is the one who is fighting for you. The same power that raised Jesus from the dead is living inside of you. When we become afraid of giving up the fight, we fail to realize that God is already fighting on our behalf. We don't have to do a single thing.

> *"If God is for us, who can be against us?"*
> *(Romans 8:31b NIV)*

God is for you. He is not mad at you; He loves you so deeply, with an everlasting love! We don't have to be afraid of letting go, because God is with us:

> *"So do not fear, for I am with you;*
> *do not be dismayed, for I am your God.*
> *I will strengthen you and help you;*
> *I will uphold you with my righteous right hand."*
> *(Isaiah 41:10 NIV)*

This is the promise we have in God.

When you don't have any energy left to fight on your own, simply be still and let go. Holy Spirit is with you in each moment; to strengthen you in your moments of weakness, to lift you up when you feel you are falling down, and to work miracles before your very eyes.

Write your prayer asking God to help you to let
go, be still, and receive from Him.

Allow Holy Spirit to speak peace and freedom
into your heart. He hears you, He knows you,
He sees you.

Ask God to give you a greater understanding of
what it truly means that He is fighting for you.

_____

_____

_____

_____

_____

_____

_____

_____

_____

_____

_____

_____

MORE TO YOU

When you feel afraid of giving up the fight, remind yourself that the battle has already been won! You can have freedom in knowing that every single day, God goes before you and prepares the way. He is already at work before you even realize it! You don't have to do anything to earn His love. You don't have to do anything for Him to fight for you.

The Lord will fight for you, you need only to be still.

God fights for you because He loves you.

There is so much more to you because God is fighting for you.

twelve: hope and a future

"I'm more than what happened to me..."
-lyric from "more to me"

In the middle of our hard days, sometimes the last thing we want to hear is "God has a plan through this." Because it doesn't feel that way at all... It feels over, it feels hard, and it feels like the end.

When you've been hurt and betrayed, it's so hard to think that there could be any good left in the world. When every day gets harder and harder, it's so hard to feel that things could ever possibly get better. When you're in the middle of your trial, completely falling apart, it can be so hard to see how God could bring anything good out of this.

The first time I read this verse after my brain injury happened, it made no sense to me:

> *"For I know the plans I have for you," declares the Lord, "plans to prosper you and not to harm you, plans to give you hope and a future."*
> *(Jeremiah 29:11 NIV)*

God has a plan? This made absolutely no sense to me because all I could see was my brain damage. All I could see were daily hospital visits. All I could see was my life in that moment. How in the world could this brain injury be part of a plan to prosper me and not to harm me? How can there be more to me when I can't even understand why this happened to me?

All I could see in front of me was the life that was taken from me. My whole family's life changed in an instant. I felt like my future was completely over because of my brain injury.

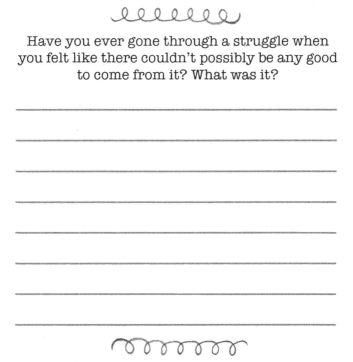

Have you ever gone through a struggle when you felt like there couldn't possibly be any good to come from it? What was it?

_____

_____

_____

_____

_____

_____

_____

_____

A HOPE AND A FUTURE

Even in the middle of my struggle, I was reading that God knows the plans He has for me. I was reading that God actually has a plan through it all. I was reading that His plans are good - plans to prosper me and not to harm me, plans to give me hope and a future. What I was reading didn't seem like my reality, but I wanted so much for it to be true. So… during the hardest time of my life, I asked God to help me understand it.

Just thinking about that now brings me to tears. I'm sitting here writing this as a college graduate, a nationally touring singer/songwriter, and a conference speaker. My life is full of things that were never dreamed possible at that time.

Even though I still have some struggles with my brain injury, years later I'm seeing that God really did have a plan.

If God had never intervened in the middle of when I had my brain injury and showed me that He had a plan for my life, I definitely would not have ever written this book… and you would not be reading it today.

> *"For I know the plans I have for you," declares the Lord, "plans to prosper you and not to harm you, plans to give you hope and a future."*
> *(Jeremiah 29:11 NIV)*

Even while you don't know what's going to happen, God knows the plans He has for you! This means that nothing comes as a surprise to Him in your life, and He's already got a way for you.

If you're going through a hard time where you can't see God's plan, please… hold on. Don't give up, because even if you can't see it right now, God is there, with plans to prosper you and not to harm you, and to bring you a hope and a future.

— WITH A LITTLE HOPE —

you can make it through today

— WITH A LITTLE FAITH —

Someday you'll get through the pain

— JUST A LITTLE LOVE —

is enough to light the way

THROUGH YOUR DARKEST NIGHT

hope

survives

♡

(lyrics from my song, "Hope Survives")

GOD LISTENS TO YOU

The next part of the verse in Jeremiah reads:

> *"Then you will call on me and come and pray to me, and I will listen to you."*
> *(Jeremiah 29:12 NIV)*

God knows that sometimes all we can see is the struggle that's right in front of us. And God understands when we feel far from Him… that's why He reminds us that He is listening. It's so amazing how when we cry out to God, He pays attention to every word.

We won't always understand or see God's plan, but we can keep going when we choose to trust Him even while not liking what's happening in our lives.

When you don't understand your circumstances, simply call out to the One who does. When you seek Him with your entire heart, you WILL find Him:

> *"You will seek me and find me when you seek me with all your heart. I will be found by you,'*
> *declares the Lord." (Jeremiah 29:13-14a NIV)*

In those hard days, cry out to Him. Seek Him with everything that you have. Tell Him all your struggles, all your fears, all your doubts… you will find Him.

Write a prayer simply calling out to God.
Say whatever comes to you in this moment.
Seek Him with all your heart.
God is listening.

_____

_____

_____

_____

_____

_____

_____

_____

_____

_____

_____

_____

_____

TAKE HEART

It's okay to feel... the tears, the pain... let it all out. Those hard days are part of your journey. God hears every one of your cries, He sees every tear you've shed, and He has heard every one of your prayers.

God is with you in every single moment:

"The Lord is a refuge for the oppressed,
a stronghold in times of trouble.
Those who know your name trust in you,
for you, Lord, have never forsaken
those who seek you." (Psalm 9:9-10 NIV)

I love how this verse simply says that God is *"a stronghold in times of trouble."* Period. It doesn't say that God is a stronghold "just in case of times of trouble"... but we have the assurance that WHEN trouble comes, God is there for us to hold onto.

God knows how we struggle and how we don't always feel like He's there. That's why He reminds us over and over in the Bible that He is with us, even in the worst of times. Take comfort in knowing that our trouble doesn't come as a surprise to God. In fact, Jesus says that we *will* have trouble in this world:

"In this world you will have trouble. But take
heart! I have overcome the world."
(John 16:33b NIV)

Right in the midst of our troubles, Jesus encourages us to "take heart"- because He has overcome the world. In His death and resurrection, Jesus was victorious over sin and death! This is not in what we have done, or will do - but in what He has already done. In those moments of struggle, Jesus is inviting you to lean on Him and trust that He will take care of you.

We can have freedom in our troubles when we remember that Jesus has already overcome for us – and because of this, we don't have to try to overcome things ourselves.

There is more to you than the troubles you face because Jesus has taken action on your behalf. Take heart! Jesus has overcome the world!

Write a prayer asking God to be your refuge
and stronghold in times of trouble.

Ask Him to help you take heart and find
freedom in not understanding and not knowing.

Ask Him to begin to reveal to you how He will
take you into your new season of a hope and a
future.

_____

_____

_____

_____

_____

_____

_____

_____

_____

_____

_____

_____

MORE TO YOU

It's okay if you are feeling stuck and you don't know what to do. In Christ, you have the freedom to feel, and you have the freedom to not know.

God is so compassionate. He understands you deeper than you know yourself. He knows you, He listens to you, and He sees you. You are not stuck. This is not the end. God is taking you on a journey; let it bring you closer to Him.

He is WITH You in your longings.

He is WITH you in this situation.

There is more to you than anything that's ever happened to you, because God has a hope and a future lined up for you.

thirteen: your story matters

"…but it's still part of my story."
-lyric from "more to me"

Some days, I feel I can take on the world. Other days, I can barely get out of bed. It's so crazy how feeling hopeless can hit out of nowhere… one moment, you feel totally fine; and the next, despair hits you and suddenly it's harder to breathe.

In those hard moments, it's so easy to begin to lose hope and to feel like our life doesn't even matter.

I know that I have felt like giving up. My thought patterns turn to anxiety, to fear, to hopelessness, and my self worth plummets because I can't see any possible way out. But… those hard moments are part of the very reason your life matters.

The very things that are holding you back right now have the potential to become the most powerful parts of your story.

YOUR STORY IS UNIQUELY YOURS

You are the only one in the entire universe with a story like yours.

Think about that! You're the only one that God has given this life. All of your days, all of your moments, all of your experiences are unique to you and only you. And because you are the only one with a story like yours… it matters. That's why your life is so significant.

Whatever has happened in your life, whatever you have felt like you couldn't escape from… know that God is with you, and He will make it part of your story. The love of God is so deep and so strong for you.

llllll

Have you ever gotten to a point where you
wanted to give up on your life story?

_____

_____

_____

_____

How does it change your perspective to know
that you are the only one with your story?

_____

_____

_____

_____

mmmmmm

the very things that are
holding you back right now
have the potential to become
the most **POWERFUL** parts
of your story.
♡

YOUR STORY HAS POWER

Your story matters more than you know. I want to share with you my absolute favorite verse about the power of our stories. It comes from the book of Revelation, which is the record of a vision the Apostle John received from the Lord on things that are to come. Here, the Lord gave John these words talking about how we, as followers of Christ, can overcome the enemy:

> *"And they overcame him by the blood of the Lamb and by the word of their testimony, and they did not love their lives to the death.'"*
> *(Revelation 12:11 NKJV)*

First, we overcome the enemy by the blood of the Lamb. Remember what we explored in section nine? The enemy is out to steal, kill, and destroy our lives. But because of the blood of Jesus, the enemy can't touch us. We have the very real power to overcome through the redemption that is ours in Jesus, which He paid for on the cross. As we read in the last section, Jesus reminds us:

> *"In this world you will have trouble. But take heart! I have overcome the world."*
> *(John 16:33b NIV)*

Jesus has already done all the hard work! We know that Jesus has paid the price and overcome death for us – we didn't do that for ourselves. That's what it means to overcome by the blood of the lamb.

The blood of the Lamb gives us the power to overcome by the word of our testimony! A testimony is your own unique story of how you personally encountered Jesus and how God helped you in your time of need.

What we have is our story of how Jesus has overcome in our life. Basically… it's your life story! Every part of it – the good and the bad. Remember how we explored the Apostle Paul's testimony in section eight (pg. 93)? In Acts 22, Paul shared where he came from and the encounter with Jesus that changed his life. As we can see from Paul's example, our testimony really does make a difference.

When we speak out the words of our testimony, we speak with power, and we don't have to be afraid or live in bondage of who we used to be. We can move forward in confidence and complete freedom in Jesus!

Think about how it feels when you share your story with someone, and they tell you how much they needed to hear it. That's part of what overcoming by the word of our testimony looks like, in practical terms! It's healing for both us and them, because in one moment, with one testimony, the enemy is overcome in two lives!

Our past no longer has power over us when we choose to speak it out. When you share your story, you completely crush the enemy!

As you speak it out, your story is no longer a stumbling block, but becomes a stepping stone to move forward. The enemy can't use your past to hurt you because you can literally overcome him by the words of your testimony! Our weapons of warfare are the words of our testimony!

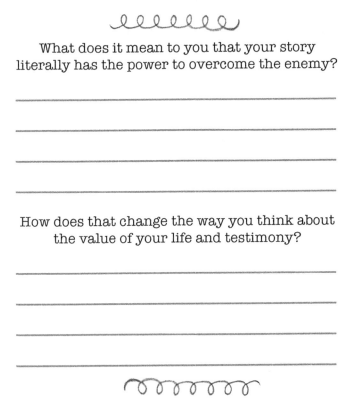

What does it mean to you that your story literally has the power to overcome the enemy?

_____

_____

_____

_____

How does that change the way you think about the value of your life and testimony?

_____

_____

_____

_____

OWNING YOUR STORY

Directly following the description of how we can overcome, the next part of the verse in Revelation says, *"and they did not love their lives to death".*

Yes, as followers of Christ we are physically not afraid to die because He gives us eternal life through His resurrection. We know we are going to Heaven to spend eternity with the Lord. But this means so much more than that.

In Christ, we have access to an entirely new life! In section eight, we talked about what it means to have a new life in Christ by the power of the Holy Spirit (pg. 92). You are a new creation:

> *"Therefore, if anyone is in Christ, the new creation has come: The old has gone, the new is here!" (2 Corinthians 5:17 NIV)*

Accepting and owning your story is one of the hardest things to do. To be able to step out and share your story with others takes so much courage. But when we recognize that we are a new creation in Christ, we can move forward in freedom! We know that we have died to our sin and our shame, and now we step confidently into freedom and grace.

We overcome the enemy when we are no longer afraid to let go of our past and step into the future that God has for us. The struggles are part of your story, but not part of your identity.

Because we have overcome the enemy, we no
longer have to hold onto our past. Pray and ask
God to show you how to begin to step forward
into the future that He has for you.

_____

_____

_____

_____

_____

_____

_____

_____

_____

_____

_____

_____

_____

_____

_____

LIVING THROUGH YOUR STORY

These verses in Psalm 40 are very special and very personal to me. The first time I read this I completely broke down, because David's words so beautifully expressed the process of living through your story:

> *"I waited patiently for the Lord;*
> *he inclined to me and heard my cry.*
> *He drew me up from the pit of destruction,*
> *out of the miry bog,*
> *and set my feet upon a rock,*
> *making my steps secure."*
> *(Psalm 40:1-2 ESV)*

David articulates his story by first sharing where he was. He describes his life as being stuck in a "pit of destruction" and a "miry bog", which is basically like a muddy swamp.

Have you felt stuck in your circumstances? David was at his darkest moment. Stuck in a life that felt like muddy, dirty, destructive pit. He couldn't do anything to get himself out of it, except wait on God and cry out to Him. It's so beautiful how in all of our hard moments, God really does care to listen to us. When we cry out to God, He listens, and He acts.

David first shares where he was, but then he shares what God did – drawing him up from the pit, setting his feet on a rock. This is beautiful imagery for what God did in David's life. God rescued David from a dark place, described as a pit of destruction. David describes how God pulled him out of the worst of circumstances and brought him into a new season of peace and security. This isn't a story of what David did for himself, but of what God did for him! The next part reads:

> "He put a new song in my mouth,
> a song of praise to our God.
> Many will see and fear,
> and put their trust in the Lord."
> (Psalm 40 1-3 ESV)

Because God brought David out of the pit, and David was willing to share his story, many lives were changed. There are 76 Psalms attributed to David. People were able to see what God did in David's life, and it encourages so many, including you and me, to know that God can do that in our lives too!

In Psalm 40,
David shares:

1. WHERE HE WAS

2. WHAT GOD DID

3. THE RESULT
   (changed lives!)

We can learn from David's example on how to overcome by the word of our testimony. Just like David talks about coming out of the pit, we can share our story and, in doing so, many lives will change as a result!

CARRYING YOUR STORY

Freedom in identity doesn't mean walking away from your story, it just means looking at it differently. There is so much more to you than what happened to you, but that doesn't discount your experiences; it only makes them that much more important. We can be shaped by our struggles without being defined by them. We can move forward in confidence, carrying our story with us every step of the way.

You can experience full freedom by knowing your identity is found in Christ. But in order to carry your story, you have to lay down your burdens.

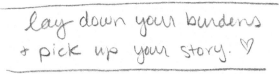

lay down your burdens + pick up your story. ♡

We can't carry our story if our hands are already full of our burdens. We can't lift our hands in praise and worship if they are weighed down by shame and guilt. But when we begin to seek the Lord… when we lift our hands up to our heavenly Father, our Abba, our Daddy, to pick us up… as we lift our hands, our burdens fall right off:

> *"Cast your burden on the Lord,*
> *and he will sustain you;*
> *he will never permit*
> *the righteous to be moved."*
> *(Psalm 55:22 ESV)*

When you cast your cares on the Lord, He will sustain you through the tears and the hard days. He will be your rock solid foundation when everything around you is shaking.

When we lay down our burdens at the feet of Jesus, we can pick up our story with confidence, knowing that God will sustain us.

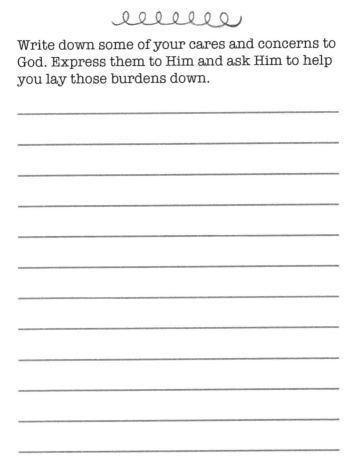

Write down some of your cares and concerns to God. Express them to Him and ask Him to help you lay those burdens down.

_____

_____

_____

_____

_____

_____

_____

_____

_____

_____

_____

Write your prayer asking God to give you the
courage to begin to step out and share
your story.

_____

_____

_____

_____

_____

_____

_____

_____

_____

_____

_____

_____

_____

_____

_____

_____

_____

MORE TO YOU

Sharing your story has so much power. . If you're struggling today, remember that God has a plan to give you a hope and a future – He already has a plan in motion to turn your test into your testimony!

Let the rivers of living water flow over you and wash off all of your shame and all of your guilt. Let the blood of Jesus wash you clean and heal your broken heart. Let God move you forward, step by step, and make all of this into part of your story.

There is more to you because your story matters.

fourteen: still on the journey

"I'm still on the journey…"
-lyric from "more to me"

Through this journey, we've explored so many different emotions.

We've explored in the Bible and looked at verses that show us how it's okay to struggle and it's okay to hurt.

We've seen how Jesus took our burdens for us, which gives us the freedom to let go and move forward.

We've seen how God is with us every step of the way.

You may not always see it, but you've come farther than you realize.

Even while reading this book, you've been on a journey.

Through the process of this journey, you've
recognized your own struggles, your own
circumstances, and your own fears.
How has recognizing some of those things about
yourself helped you?

_____

_____

_____

_____

_____

_____

_____

_____

_____

_____

_____

_____

_____

FINDING STRENGTH IN JESUS

Freedom in identity doesn't mean that you'll never struggle. I love these words of the Apostle Paul about being content in all situations:

> *"I know what it is to be in need, and I know what it is to have plenty. I have learned the secret of being content in any and every situation, whether well fed or hungry, whether living in plenty or in want. I can do all this through him who gives me strength." (Philippians 4:12-13)*

Our circumstances can be hard. Our emotions can get out of control. But through it all, our constant is found in the love of Christ.

No matter what your life looks like right now, you can have hope and security in knowing that God is with you every single day. God has a plan for your life and is fighting for you before you even realize it.

When you fall, He's there to pick you back up. When you cry, He's there to comfort your heart. In your weakest moments, Jesus gives you strength!

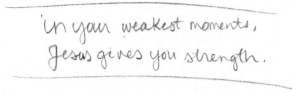

In your weakest moments,
Jesus gives you strength.

When you feel at your weakest, Jesus is there to be your strength. How does that change your perspective in the hard moments?

_____

_____

_____

_____

_____

_____

_____

_____

_____

_____

_____

_____

_____

_____

_____

_____

GOD IS ALWAYS WITH YOU

God is with you every single step of your journey.

> *"When you pass through the waters, I will be with you; and through the rivers, they shall not overwhelm you; when you walk through fire you shall not be burned, and the flame shall not consume you."*
> *(Isaiah 43:2 ESV)*

Read that passage again, thinking about the struggles you face in your life. No matter how hard it gets, God promises to always be with us. We have the power that raised Jesus from the dead inside of us by the Holy Spirit – and God will enable us to get through it all.

Freedom in identity doesn't mean you'll never struggle; it simply comes from knowing who you are in Jesus. It comes from knowing that you have overcome so much through Christ. We have the freedom to step out knowing that our story really matters.

freedom in identity simply comes from knowing who you are in Jesus.

What are some ways you've recognized God has
been with you on your journey while reading
this book?

_____

_____

_____

_____

_____

_____

_____

What have you learned about your identity
found in the price Jesus paid for you? How does
that impact the way you see yourself?

_____

_____

_____

_____

_____

_____

_____

STILL ON THE JOURNEY

The love of God is big enough to cover all of your hurts, all of your failures, all of your mistakes. God is big enough to handle all of your tears, heal all of your aches, and give you rest during all of your sleepless nights. His love is powerful and beautiful, and it drives out all of your fears.

It's okay if you don't always know how to move forward - you are still on the journey. Life with Christ doesn't mean you have it all together... it just means that you have Someone else to rely on in those moments!

You will continue to grow, learn, and experience more of God each and every day of your life! Remember that the same power that raised Jesus from the dead is inside of YOU! You have access to the power of the fullness of God through the Holy Spirit!

Jesus says to come as you are. When you are having a bad day, come, lay your burdens down, and let Him take the heavy load off your heart.

There is so much more to you than everything
that has happened to you. Knowing the
freedom you have in Jesus, make the decision
right now to own your story!

Write a prayer asking God to help you carry
your testimony and share it with others.

_____

_____

_____

_____

_____

_____

_____

_____

_____

_____

_____

_____

_____

_____

MORE TO YOU

Once you put this book down, make the decision to move forward with freedom, knowing your identity is secure in God's love for you. Some days will be hard and some days will be good. But you have access to freedom through every single day of your life!

Always remember that you are not alone and your life has purpose.

There is so much more to you!

there is
more to you.

♡

about the author

 **Cristabelle Braden** is a singer, songwriter, speaker on brain injury, and the founder of Hope After Head Injury. After suffering a traumatic brain injury as a young teen, she has grown and overcome barriers that were never dreamed possible, including graduating from college, writing and recording original music, and touring the country as a singer and speaker on brain injury. She never wrote a song before the brain injury, but within the first month of recovery songs started pouring out of her. All of this has given Cristabelle a great resolve to use music to share her hope-filled story of rehabilitation from brain injury as a way to encourage and empower others going through similar circumstances.

In 2017, she released an original EP entitled *Hope Survives*, and has toured all over the country to sing and speak at churches, conferences, brain injury support groups, hospitals, rehab centers, prison ministries, homeless shelters, music venues, and more. She is also an established speaker and has given the keynote address at brain injury conferences across the nation, including the Mayo Clinic and multiple statewide Brain Injury Associations. The goal of her organization Hope After Head Injury is to provide a support system which focuses on the emotional aspect on healing from brain injury, with an emphasis on online support. *www.CristabelleBraden.com*

CRISTABELLE WOULD LOVE TO MEET YOU!

TOUR DATES AT **CRISTABELLEBRADEN.COM**

BOOK HER TO SING, SPEAK, OR LEAD WORSHIP AT
YOUR CHURCH, CONFERENCE, WOMEN'S GROUP,
YOUTH GROUP, SUPPORT GROUP, OR EVENT!

EMAIL: **BOOKING@CRISTABELLEBRADEN.COM**

HOPE. SUPPORT. ENCOURAGEMENT. AWARENESS.

JOIN THE COMMUNITY >>

FOUNDED BY CRISTABELLE BRADEN

Living with brain injury can be very scary when you're stuck in the middle of confusion, you feel like nobody understands, and you don't know what to do. But you don't have to fight this battle alone. There are millions of people who have experienced brain injury and understand what you are going through. Some days are harder than others... but there is always hope!

· LIVE BRAIN INJURY ENCOURAGEMENT CHATS

Join founder Cristabelle Braden for a weekly live video support chat!
Comment along live with other survivors and caregivers.
HOW: TUESDAYS @ 7pm Eastern on our Facebook Page

· ONLINE SUPPORT GROUP

Separate from our public page, this is a closed (not public) and moderated group which provides a way to share and connect with others in the brain injury community.
HOW: join - facebook.com/groups/hopeafterheadinjury

· SHARE YOUR STORY

We love to share survivor & caregiver stories and quotes on our social media & blog - to show how we are not alone, and to give survivors a voice. Read stories & share yours!
HOW: submit to info@hopeafterheadinjury.com

· COME TO AN EVENT (or invite Cristabelle!)

Hope After Head Injury founder Cristabelle Braden speaks and sings across the country, and would love to meet you! Bring her to your support group or attend a scheduled event.
HOW: event schedule at cristabellebraden.com

· CONNECT ON SOCIAL MEDIA

Share posts with #hopeafterheadinjury to spread the hope & join our online community:
HOW: search "Hope After Head Injury" on Facebook / Instagram

HOPEAFTERHEADINJURY.COM

Made in the USA
Middletown, DE
30 March 2019